LET'S TALK ABOUT

THE TRANSLATION OF THE BOOK OF MORMON

OTHER BOOKS IN THE
LET'S TALK ABOUT SERIES

Let's Talk about Polygamy

Let's Talk about Religion and Mental Health

Let's Talk about the Book of Abraham

Let's Talk about Faith and Intellect

Let's Talk about the Law of Consecration

Let's Talk about Temples and Ritual

Let's Talk about Race and Priesthood

For more information on the other books
in the Let's Talk About series,
visit DesBook.com/LetsTalk.

LET'S TALK ABOUT

THE TRANSLATION OF THE BOOK OF MORMON

**GERRIT J. DIRKMAAT
MICHAEL HUBBARD MACKAY**

SALT LAKE CITY, UTAH

© 2023 Gerrit J. Dirkmaat and Michael Hubbard MacKay

All rights reserved. No part of this book may be reproduced in any form or by any means without permission in writing from the publisher, Deseret Book Company, at permissions@deseretbook.com. This work is not an official publication of The Church of Jesus Christ of Latter-day Saints. The views expressed herein are the responsibility of the authors and do not necessarily represent the position of the Church, of Brigham Young University, or of Deseret Book Company.

DESERET BOOK is a registered trademark of Deseret Book Company.

Visit us at deseretbook.com

Library of Congress Cataloging-in-Publication Data
CIP on file
ISBN 978-1-63993-091-3

Printed in the United States of America
PubLitho, Draper, UT

10 9 8 7 6 5 4 3 2 1

To Gail Miller.

Her efforts have done more to advance the understanding of Latter-day Saint history than any other person in the twenty-first century.

CONTENTS

Introduction: Of Men and Miracles 1

1. Visions and Failures 9

2. Marrying Emma and Obtaining the Plates 18

3. Early Translation with Emma and Martin, 1828 . . . 25

4. Loss Precedes the Miracle 37

5. Finishing the Work 48

6. How Did Joseph Translate
   the Book of Mormon? 62

7. Important Questions and Possible Answers 80

Conclusion 108

Further Reading 111

Notes 113

Index 127

INTRODUCTION

OF MEN AND MIRACLES

In August 1829, newspaper editor Jonathan Hadley was angry at Joseph Smith. Joseph had recently approached Hadley and Egbert Grandin, rival editors in Palmyra, a few weeks earlier with the prospect of publishing the Book of Mormon. Grandin, who competed with Hadley for readers and was his political rival, had already vigorously refused to publish the book. Grandin published in his paper his disdain for the entire project, calling Joseph Smith's account of gold plates "a pretended discovery."[1] Unlike his nemesis Grandin, Hadley had not rejected the project outright. But Hadley's small facilities were totally inadequate to publish the nearly six-hundred-page book, especially at a print run of five thousand copies. Possibly hoping to still share in the profits from publication, Hadley had referred Joseph and Martin to his mentor and friend, Thurlow Weed, in Rochester. Though Joseph Smith and Martin Harris tried, they were unable to convince Weed to publish the book. However, with an agreement with another Rochester publisher in hand, Joseph returned to Palmyra and was able to convince Grandin to relent in his opposition and publish the Book of Mormon.

When Hadley learned that it would not be his friend but his chief competitor publishing the Book of Mormon and that thousands of Martin Harris's dollars would be pouring into Egbert Grandin's coffers, Hadley reacted in anger and lashed out at Joseph Smith. Hadley's chief weapon was always his biting, sarcastic wit, which he used to pillory politician and religionist alike when they crossed him. And Joseph Smith had now crossed him. Hadley published a lengthy attack on the "Gold Bible" in his newspaper, repeating the story of the discovery of the gold plates and Joseph Smith's explanation of the miraculous translation.

Unlike later antagonists of Joseph Smith, Hadley did little to attack Joseph Smith personally. He did not need to. Anyone who heard Joseph's story of angelic visitations, ancient plates, holy devices used to translate them, and receiving revelations from God would, Hadley assumed, immediately reject the whole idea as preposterous. Without the manuscript in his hand, Hadley particularly scoffed at the idea that Joseph Smith could even produce such a book—one that proclaimed itself to be another book of scripture, equal if not superior to the Holy Bible itself. After all, Joseph Smith was, Hadley asserted, "very illiterate." As fantastical as Joseph's story of the angel sounded, the idea that this uneducated farm boy translated the purported book from ancient records seemed even more implausible to Hadley.

At the time Hadley published his dismissive article, there were few indications to him or anyone else that Joseph Smith or the Book of Mormon would amount to anything more than a curiosity that would quickly be lost in the rapidly shifting sands of time. There was not yet a Church of Christ (the original name of The Church of Jesus Christ of Latter-day Saints), and it would not be organized for another eight months. In Palmyra, where Hadley lived, only Joseph Smith's own family seemed to have accepted Joseph's claims. The lone exception was Martin Harris, whom even Hadley in his criticism seemed perplexed about because Harris was "an honest and industrious farmer," well respected in the community. Harris notwithstanding, Hadley dismissed Joseph's claims and the Book of Mormon, believing that they would be rejected entirely by anyone who heard the story or read the book.[2]

But Hadley could not have been more wrong about the impact of both Joseph Smith and the Book of Mormon. He had not read the Book of Mormon, but within only a few years of its publication, thousands of people did read it. These men and women believed it to be scripture and its translator, the "illiterate" Joseph Smith, to be a seer and a prophet. As more and more people came to believe that the Book of Mormon was another testament of Christ, efforts to explain its origin increased, diversified, and became more caustic and desperate.

From the beginning, the Book of Mormon was the central piece of evidence to Joseph Smith's claims that he had indeed been called of God. This radical belief that God had called a new prophet and through him brought forth new scripture and restored the original Church of Jesus Christ was so connected with its members that first detractors, and then soon everyone, labeled the sect with the appellation stemming from the book: Mormons. Joseph Smith declared the Book of Mormon to be the keystone of the Latter-day Saint religion, and every leader of the Church since his death has again affirmed the Book of Mormon's central place in Latter-day Saint belief and theology. As such, over the nearly two centuries since its publication, the Book of Mormon has undergone intense scrutiny, both by those seeking to dismiss it or provide an alternate explanation for its origin and by believers seeking greater spiritual guidance from it.

For his part, Joseph Smith always maintained that the translation of the Book of Mormon was a miracle. He affirmed that "through the medium of the Urim and Thummim," he had "translated the record by the gift and power of God."[3]

As soon as believers and skeptics were able to peruse the book's pages, they set forth explanations for *how* it was produced. Believers added details to Joseph's description of the process of translation. Meanwhile, skeptics offered explanations for how Joseph Smith either attempted to pawn off someone else's prose as a miracle or had himself creatively produced a fiction. Thus, even before it was published (and even more so afterward), the Book of Mormon became the focal point of those joining or deriding the Church of Christ. Many offered their own explanations of how the Book of Mormon came into being. Those various explanations often did not take the accounts Joseph and his scribes gave at face value. Some attempted to prove it was not a miracle, while others would later embellish the events to try to make it seem more miraculous. In either case, the explanations did not describe the miracle as the participants said that it happened.

Historians always worry about making an event into something that it was not. This is especially so when writing about miracles. Throughout the ages, many men and women have claimed to have experienced revelations or miraculous visitations from God or angels. Historians generally do not examine the claims of these people to determine whether or not they actually had contact with God or the divine in some way. For example, the synoptic Gospels (Matthew, Mark, and Luke) all document an event in which Jesus walked on water. The New Testament is a historical document that historians use and analyze. In this historical document individual authors express their belief that Jesus walked on water, yet it is beyond the scope of historical inquiry to determine whether or not Jesus *actually* walked on water. It would be even more difficult for a historian to determine precisely how Jesus walked on water. Historians can only establish, through documents, what most likely happened in the past. They have no ability to prove or test whether or not a miracle actually occurred. How could you prove that Jesus Christ walked on water? One could theoretically test millions of people to see if they could prove that biblical miracle by asking them to try to do the same. However, such an experiment is likely to end up all wet. None of the volunteers would walk on water as Jesus or Peter did. Would that prove that Jesus did not walk on water? No. Because when Jesus walked on water, He did it by the power of God, and no scientist or theorist can force the replication of that divine force.

In any case, attempts to explain or deny such miraculous claims diminish the authors' intended purpose. In fact, the entire point of the authors of the gospels was to assert the reality of that miracle and the many other miracles of Jesus. No matter how convincing any analysis to prove or disprove the miracle is, the Gospel of Matthew still records the author's expression of belief that those miracles did in fact occur. That cannot change.

So what can a historian do? He or she can definitively say, "Jesus's followers certainly believed that Jesus walked on water." That is a statement of fact that neither dismisses the potential of a divine miracle, however unlikely, nor affirms it in a provable way. If someone responds, "Well, I find it hard to believe that Jesus actually walked on water," the reality is that it is more than hard to believe; the event is impossible without the intervention of God. In fact, that is precisely what a miracle is: something that could not occur without the power of God intervening. That a miracle is hard to believe because it cannot be replicated by the scientific world is actually the reason believers revere miracles so deeply. People cannot call fire down from heaven, people do not walk on water, and the dead do not come out of their tombs alive again; except when they do. And the story of Christianity is the belief that the greatest miracle ever recorded—the death and Resurrection of Jesus Christ for the remission of the world's sins—is indeed true, whether it can be scientifically proven or not.

Joseph Smith's miraculous claims are similar to those of the New Testament. Joseph Smith wrote that the Book of Mormon was produced by the "Gift and Power of God." This assertion was published in the preface of the 1830 edition of the Book of Mormon. What happens if we take this statement at face value? What happens if we carefully analyze the translation of the Book of Mormon historically, avoiding analysis that makes it either more than it is or less than a miracle? Would we understand the translation of the Book of Mormon better?

In 2013, The Church of Jesus Christ of Latter-day Saints published a Gospel Topics essay entitled "Book of Mormon Translation." This essay used the historical sources to describe the translation process as Joseph, Emma, Martin, Oliver, David, and other key witnesses described it. This book will expand upon that brief essay to examine these and other sources in greater detail.

Emma Smith

Martin Harris

Oliver Cowdery

David Whitmer

Lucy Mack Smith

In relating the story of the translation of the Book of Mormon, this book draws on explanations from Joseph Smith as well as the accounts of those who witnessed the translation—namely, Emma Smith, Martin Harris, Oliver Cowdery, David Whitmer, and Lucy Mack Smith.

All images public domain

Thus, this book will describe how Joseph Smith obtained and then translated the gold plates, using Joseph Smith's own explanations and the accounts of witnesses, scribes, and close friends who left records about those events. It will strip back the synthetic analysis that tries to demonstrate or denigrate the miracle of the translation of the Book of Mormon. It will take the translation at face value, as it was described by those closest to Joseph and especially by those who watched it happen. We give preference to the statements and historical documentation left by Joseph Smith and witnesses Emma Smith, Oliver Cowdery, Martin Harris, David Whitmer, and Lucy Mack Smith. We do not give preference to those nonwitnesses who dismissed the translation's miraculous nature. This does not mean that we will not be critical of the sources; in fact, we challenge witnesses of the translation when they extend their own analysis about what happened—including when Emma, Martin, and David claimed they knew what Joseph Smith saw on his seer stones. We will make sense of these documents by placing them within historical context. We hope that by placing these accounts in the narrative of the story of the translation from 1827 to 1829, readers will better understand them and how they relate to one another. Though we have examined many of these sources in person in the archives, we will provide, when possible, citations to where these documents can be accessed online or to published versions, primarily from the Joseph Smith Papers and the Church History Library websites.

This book will first explain the events that occurred after Joseph experienced his visions and then obtained the plates. It will then describe the events that took place during the translation of the Book of Mormon. Next, the book will examine how the Book of Mormon was translated, according to witnesses. Finally, we will attempt to answer common questions Latter-day Saints have about the translation of the Book of Mormon.

This book expands upon the historical explanation found in the Gospel Topics essays, but readers should be aware that other faithful Latter-day Saints have proffered different theories about the translation of the Book of Mormon, which attempt to describe the process in different ways. But this book addresses common questions that arise in light of the *historical* explanation of the miracle of translation, and those subscribing to different theories of translation will no doubt find some of our questions and answers unsatisfying.

The witnesses of translation, along with Joseph Smith, all declared the gold plates to be real and tangible. They also described Joseph's use of sacred stones as part of the miraculous translation process. Their accounts of that process, and their fervent testimonies of the Book of Mormon's truthfulness, will help readers understand the translation as they understood it. They uniformly believed that the translation was indeed a miracle from God. This same belief is held by millions of Latter-day Saints today. We hope that, through this book, those believers will better understand what the historical sources have to say about the translation of the Book of Mormon and the events surrounding that process.

CHAPTER 1

VISIONS AND FAILURES

For us as Latter-day Saints, the miraculous vision Joseph Smith experienced in 1820 is part of the bedrock of our belief. Indeed, in 2020, on the two-hundredth anniversary of his vision, the First Presidency and Quorum of the Twelve Apostles issued a proclamation affirming Joseph Smith's central role in the Restoration of Jesus Christ's "New Testament Church." The leaders declared, "In answer to his prayer, God the Father and His Son, Jesus Christ, appeared to Joseph and inaugurated the 'restitution of all things' as foretold in the Bible."[1]

During the twenty-four years after the First Vision, Joseph experienced numerous visitations from heavenly messengers and received from them various powers, teachings, and authorities, and he established a restored Church of Jesus Christ on the earth. In the process, Joseph received dozens of revelations, many of which would come to be published in the Doctrine and Covenants. These heavenly ministers and divine revelations greatly expanded the understanding of Joseph and those who would come to join the restored Church.

As new revelation illuminated a theological path that had long been darkened by sectarian overgrowth, Joseph Smith abandoned many standard Christian beliefs shared across most sects and denominations. For instance, he would come to disregard the traditional Christian idea that God has no body, parts, or passions, instead teaching that He was in fact a corporeal, exalted man. Even further, Joseph revealed that men and women were themselves, in fact, eternal beings, capable of becoming like God, though always worshipping Him.

Coupled with Joseph's expansive teachings on heaven, hell, postmortal salvation, and premortal life, Latter-day Saint theology burst onto the Christian world as perhaps the most radical thunderstorm to emerge from the maelstrom of the Second Great Awakening.

Because Joseph Smith served as the revelator of so many teachings about God and Jesus Christ that many Latter-day Saints deeply treasure, it can be easy to forget the slow process whereby he obtained his knowledge. Modern Latter-day Saints might assume that Joseph understood the entirety of the Restoration from the beginning, in 1820 or 1830. Brigham Young attempted to disabuse Latter-day Saints in early Utah Territory of this idea that Joseph received much, if not all, of his knowledge at once. Explaining the process of continuing revelation, Brigham Young declared, "The Lord can't reveal to you and I that we can't understand; . . . for instance when Joseph first received revelation the Lord could not tell him what he was going to do. He didn't tell him he was going to call him to be a prophet, seer, revelator, high priest, and founder of [the] kingdom of God on earth. Joseph would have said . . . [']just what does that mean? You are talking that I can t understand.[']" Instead, President Young explained that, at the beginning, God "could merely reveal to him [Joseph] that the Lord was pleased to bless him and forgive his sins and there was a work for him to perform on the earth and that was about all he could reveal."[2]

Rather than emerging from the Sacred Grove with his prophetic life and mission laid out before him, Joseph learned only step-by-step what God would have him do, particularly regarding the translation of the gold plates, which contained the Book of Mormon. Brigham Young further described these early days:

> The first time he [God] sent [an] angel to visit him [Joseph] he could then lead his mind a little further. He could reveal to him there was certain records deposited in the earth to be brought forth for the benefit of [the]

inhabitants of the earth. He could reveal after this that Joseph could get them; then he could reveal he should have power to translate the records from the language and characters in which it was written and give it to the people in the English language, but this was not taught him first. . . . He could then tell him he was to be called a prophet. He could then reveal to Joseph that he might take Oliver Cowdery into water and baptize him and ordain him to [the] priesthood. After this he could tell him he could receive the high priesthood to organize the church and so on. . . . This is the way the Lord has to instruct all people upon the earth. I make mention of this to show you that . . . the Lord can't teach all things to people at once. He gives a little here [a] little there, revelation upon revelation, . . . revelation after revelation, a precept today, tomorrow another, next day another. If the people make good use of it and improve upon what the Lord gives them, then he is ready to bestow more.[3]

The process whereby Joseph obtained the gold plates was certainly one of wonder, but it was also marred by halting progress and clear frustration, and in context of the teenage boy's life, it must have been painfully slow.

In his own words, Joseph explained that in the weeks and months that followed his first powerful vision of the divine, "I fell into transgressions and sinned in many things which brought a wound upon my soul."[4] In another account he remembered, "I was left to all kinds of temptations, and mingling with all kinds of society. . . . I frequently fell into many foolish errors and displayed the weakness of youth and the corruption of human nature."[5]

Joseph never elaborated on what these teenage transgressions were. Perhaps he had in mind his association with those who believed they could find buried treasure or gold or silver deposits. Working to provide for the family was constantly on the minds of the entire Smith family. They were so desperately poor that Joseph and his brothers regularly hired out their labor, an act that lessened the family's social standing in New York. In the culture of the agrarian Northeast, families that were forced to hire out their children to make ends meet demonstrated a lack of what was termed "competency," or the ability to enjoy a comfortable living simply by working and laboring on one's own lands.[6] Lucy Mack Smith, Joseph's mother, recalled that when the family arrived in Palmyra, they were "almost destitute of money, property, or acquaintances."[7] They would struggle for years without success to fully overcome their poverty and indebtedness.

Joseph's visitation from Moroni came in the context of this daily struggle with poverty and guilt over his personal failings. He explained, "When I was seventeen years of age I called again upon the Lord and he shewed unto me a heavenly vision for behold an angel of the Lord came and stood before me and it was by night and he called me by name."[8] Joseph recalled that the light was so bright that it was as if the house was on fire, and "the appearance produced a shock that affected the whole body."[9]

Perhaps even more shocking to the seventeen-year-old was the message delivered by the angel. To his relief, his sins were forgiven. But immediately another message was delivered, both exhilarating and terrifying in its importance. Joseph explained that the angel told him "there was plates of gold upon which there was engravings which was engraven by Maroni [Moroni] & his fathers the servants of the living God in ancient days and deposited by the commandments of God and kept by the power thereof and that I should go and get them."[10] As the angel described the plates, Joseph's mind was opened to another vision of the spot where the plates were buried.

However, it was not just the plates the angel described as awaiting Joseph's discovery. The angel also told him of other buried ancient relics, including a device that Joseph referred to as "spectacles for to read the book."[11] The angel declared to Joseph that this "Urim & Thummim was hid up with the record, and that God would give [him] power to translate it with the assistance of this instrument."[12] The angel explained the

VISIONS AND FAILURES

device consisted of "two stones in silver bows."[13] (For more on the Urim and Thummim, see chapter 3.)

After delivering numerous teachings and quoting many scriptures, the angel pronounced a dire warning: "He told me that when I got those plates of which he had spoken. . . . I should not show them to any person, neither the breastplate with the Urim and Thummim only to those to whom I should be commanded to show them, If I did I should be destroyed."[14]

While the angel impressed upon him both teachings and warnings, Joseph's mind was taken away in a vision of the place where these sacred objects were buried, not far from his home; this vision was so vibrant that Joseph related, "I could see the place where the plates were deposited and that so clearly and distinctly that I knew the place again when I visited it."[15]

The angel's message was of such great import that he returned two more times in the course of the sleepless night, each time recounting and reinforcing the previous instructions and elaborating on others. After a draining and totally restless, miracle-filled night, Joseph attempted to work the family farm as usual, but could not. Lucy Smith explained that while her son was reaping wheat with his older brother Alvin and their father, Joseph paused. Alvin urged his little brother to continue the work or else they would "not be able to complete [their] task." Joseph dutifully attempted to resume their arduous work. However, exhaustion overcame him, and he again stopped. This time his father grew concerned that Joseph must be sick and instructed him to return home to his mother to be cared for. Joseph began to make his way back, but by the time he reached the shade of a nearby apple tree, he could go no further and collapsed on the ground.[16]

Rather than receiving the respite of sleep, Joseph was again startled by the same angel, who not only rehearsed the same information but also chastised Joseph for not informing his father of the visions as he had been told. Any number of reasons might have prevented the young Joseph from disclosing the miraculous encounters. Possibly remembering the stinging rebuke he had received when he dutifully recounted his First Vision to a Methodist preacher he'd admired, Joseph may have initially hesitated to involve his family further in his experiences with divine manifestations.

Perhaps the weight of what the angel had told him exacerbated that fear. Unlike his First Vision, which contained only a message of forgiveness and hope for the future, the angel now declared to Joseph, in no uncertain terms, that he would be despised by the world. Further, the angel had commanded Joseph to protect the plates, suggesting he would have to face those who would try to steal them. Whatever the reason Joseph hesitated to tell his father at first, faced with this latest angelic injunction, Joseph did as directed and sought out his father to tell him of the fantastic experience. Joseph remembered his father's total embrace of his son's easily unbelievable tale. "The old man wept," Joseph recalled, "and told me that it was a vision from God, and to attend to it."[17]

His exhaustion temporarily gone, Joseph made his way to the hill the angel had shown him in vision in order to get the plates as he had been directed. The astounding events of the previous twenty-four hours, his exhilaration combined with fatigue, must have left the young man with many conflicting thoughts and emotions as he climbed the hill.

When he came to the spot, he recognized it instantly from the vision of the previous night. He then opened the stone box to reveal its millennia-old relics. Inside the box he saw the gold plates, a breastplate, and two stones fastened together in a device that somewhat resembled spectacles, though they were much larger and had stones rather than glass lenses.[18]

Only those who have known the biting sting of poverty will be able to fully relate with the wave of feelings that crashed down over Joseph Smith as he gazed down at the dozens of pounds of gold plates. The multiple angelic warnings receded behind the immediate, obvious reality of what Joseph had found. Gold! These plates would be worth thousands

VISIONS AND FAILURES

The Hill Cumorah, where Joseph communed with an angel and eventually obtained the gold plates, as it appears today.

upon thousands of dollars. Indeed, one leaf of the plates would likely have sufficed to settle all of the Smith family debts and place them finally on the road to financial stability and community respect. No more would his mother need to worry and be forced to sell rags to make ends meet; no more would his father feel the societal weight of being regarded as an abject failure because his sons were forced to hire out their labor on others' farms. How much did the plates weigh? Were they solid gold? Perhaps just breaking off a piece of them would help his family financially while still preserving the record.[19]

Whatever exact thoughts flooded his seventeen-year-old mind, Joseph had clearly begun contemplating the potential monetary windfall to some degree as he reached into the box to grab hold of them. Oliver Cowdery later reflected on what went through Joseph's mind, as Joseph had explained it to him: "Two invisible powers were operating upon his mind during his walk from his residence to Cumorah . . . the one urging the certainty of wealth and ease in this life."[20]

But as Joseph attempted to take possession of the treasure in front of him, he found himself prevented by some unseen yet incredibly powerful force. He tried a second time. Again, he could not grab the plates. After a third failed attempt, Joseph explained that he became "exceedingly frightened."

As he had the night before, and as he had in the Sacred Grove three years earlier, Joseph said he "cried unto the Lord in the agony of my soul why can I not obtain them." The stillness of the trees around him miraculously shattered as the same angel again appeared to the exhausted, pleading, frustrated, and scared teenager. The angel delivered both information and reproof: "You have not kept the commandments of the Lord which I gave unto you," the angel declared. "Therefore you cannot now obtain them for the time is not yet fulfilled therefore thou wast left unto temptation that thou mightest be made accquainted of with the power of the adversary."[21]

The stinging rebuke must have been overwhelming to Joseph. He had distinctly failed, despite having seen God and Jesus Christ a few years earlier and despite being commissioned by an angel from heaven with a mission in four separate miraculous manifestations. In the moment, Satan's temptation to view the plates for their earthly worth rather than their heavenly pricelessness had overcome Joseph. With grave honesty he confessed his sin to the world: "I had been tempted of the adversary and sought the Plates to obtain riches and kept not the commandment that I should have an eye single to the Glory of God."[22]

But with the heavenly reprimand, the angel also provided him hope once again. He commanded, "Repent and call on the Lord thou shalt be forgiven and in his own due time thou shalt obtain them."[23] Joseph was further instructed to return to the same spot in a full year and the angel would meet with him again.

These annual conversations with the angel occurred for three more years, and each time Joseph left without the plates since he still was not personally prepared to obtain them. As he explained in his later history, throughout those years the family's struggle with poverty meant Joseph had to work many hard hours of manual labor: "As my father's worldly circumstances were very, limited we were under the necessity of laboring with our hands, hiring by days works and otherwise as we could get opportunity."[24]

After four abortive excursions to obtain the gold plates, however, Joseph returned a fifth time in September 1827, having had a major change in the focus of his life. Seven years had passed since the fourteen-year-old Joseph had first feared that the trees around him were about to catch fire as the indescribable light of his First Vision rested upon him. His years of angelic visitations that followed no doubt helped focus and transform Joseph, but nothing seems to have had as much effect on him as his chance meeting with Emma Hale Smith.

CHAPTER 2

MARRYING EMMA AND OBTAINING THE PLATES

In his efforts to hire out his labor to support his family, Joseph agreed to work for Josiah Stowell, who believed he knew the location of an abandoned Spanish silver mine in northern Pennsylvania. Harmony was roughly 150 miles away from his family home in the Palmyra area, so Joseph needed to find a local Harmony resident to board with. Finding a place with the family of Isaac and Elizabeth Hale, nineteen-year-old Joseph met Emma, their twenty-one-year-old daughter. Very little is known about Joseph and Emma's interactions with one another prior to their marriage, except that Isaac Hale, Emma's father, was absolutely opposed to their relationship. The two came from completely different circumstances and worlds. The Hales were well-off, well-respected, and grounded in their Methodist faith. Joseph Smith was from a poor family, had little education, and worked as a day laborer digging for an apparently mythical silver mine because local folklorists believed he had special abilities that would help him find buried treasure. Worse, as their association continued, Joseph likely described his miraculous visions and what must have seemed to Isaac Hale tall tales of buried gold plates that he had seen but not yet obtained.[1]

Even after Joseph stopped boarding at the Hale home, he returned several times to visit Emma. Eventually, Joseph decided that he wanted to marry Emma. Lucy Mack Smith recalled that Joseph came to her and confided that he had been "very lonely ever since Alvin died." Shifting quickly from the somber to the celebratory, he told his mother, "I have concluded to get married." He then explained that, if he had his parents' blessing, "Miss Emma Hale would be my choice before any other woman I have ever seen." The Smiths readily embraced the match and even encouraged Joseph to bring Emma back to Palmyra to live with them once they were wed.[2]

While the Smiths exulted in the possibility of a marriage between Joseph and Emma, the Hales were a different matter entirely. Joseph eventually worked up the courage to ask the taciturn Isaac Hale for permission to marry his daughter. Hale flatly rejected the request. He later bitterly explained, "[Joseph Smith] asked my consent to his marrying my daughter Emma. This I refused, and gave my reasons for so doing some of which were, that he was a stranger, and followed a business that I could not approve." And Hale's acrimony only grew with what happened next. Though he had put his foot down and seemingly ended their courtship, Hale explained, "Not long after this, he [Joseph] returned, and while I was absent from home, carried off my daughter, into the state of New York, where they were married without my approbation or consent."[3]

Hale's version of the story reflects either his misunderstanding of the events or a deliberate attempt to obfuscate and place all of the blame on Joseph Smith instead of recognizing the role of his daughter, Emma. Rather than Joseph coming to the Hale home as the proverbial thief in the night and "carrying off" Emma for a clandestine marriage rendezvous, the event was described by Emma very differently.

Emma explained that she had gone to Bainbridge, New York, to visit Josiah Stowell's household; she does not indicate if she did so because she knew Joseph had planned to come there. Whether she arrived by some kind of prearrangement with Joseph Smith or if it was just happenstance, Joseph called while she was there, and the two were reunited following her father's adamant rejection of Joseph. Emma acknowledged, "My folks were bitterly opposed to him." Sensing this might be their only opportunity, Joseph urged Emma to marry him then and there.[4]

Though she clearly had some affinity for Joseph, Emma recalled, "I had no intention of marrying when I left home." While their early relationship is often romanticized by twenty-first-century Saints who want to see something of their own modern American courtship and marriage in this early nineteenth-century one, Emma was apparently not blinded by romantic love nor desperate to be with her one-and-only Joseph. She recalled with great candor, "[Joseph] urged me to marry him, and preferring to marry him to any other man I knew, I consented." Weighing her options, Emma knew that if she returned home, she would likely be pressured into a marriage that was much more her father's preference than hers. Isaac Hale had already blocked at least one suitor. Living in the sparsely populated Harmony area, Emma no doubt knew very well what men her parents deemed to be worthy future spouses, and she, like many other women in that bigoted and male-dominated society, chose to exercise what agency she had and vote with her feet, or in this case, her marriage vow. If she was to marry, it would at least be with someone she "preferred."[5] Her decision not only greatly impacted the remainder of Joseph's life but also was key to the unfolding Restoration of the gospel.

Rather than returning to Harmony to face the unknown, but certainly uncomfortable, reaction from Isaac Hale at their sudden elopement, the newlyweds traveled up to Joseph's family home in Palmyra, where Lucy Mack Smith had already opened welcome arms to them.

Not long after they arrived together in Palmyra, Joseph's years-long odyssey to obtain the gold plates became even more intense. The plates still lay buried in the hill, awaiting the day when Joseph's personal worthiness matched the gravity of the sacred task he was to be entrusted with. While journeying past the hill one day, Joseph was detained. His parents, worried that he had not returned when expected, feared that someone had perhaps attacked or harmed their son. Anxious hours passed until "the night was far spent." Finally, an exhausted

Joseph made his way into the home and collapsed into a chair, unable to speak for lack of energy for some time. Joseph Smith Sr. tried multiple times to get an explanation from his son, who finally related: "I have taken the severest chastisement that I have ever had in my life." His fatherly instincts on full display, Joseph Smith Sr. became instantly angry. "Who has spoken to my son this way?!" he thought and demanded to know of Joseph upon whom he could direct his rising ire.[6]

Joseph attempted to calm his father and explained that the chastisement he had received was not from any mortal but from "the angel of the Lord." Joseph explained that on his way to the hill, he had been met by the angel, who told him, in part, "that I had not been engaged enough in the work of the Lord; that the time had come for the record to be brought forth; and, that I must be up and doing, and set myself about the things which God had commanded me to do."[7]

Whatever transpired in the months that followed, when the time for his annual meeting with the angel arrived again on September 22, 1827, Joseph had, with Emma's help, at last prepared himself for what was to be an awesome responsibility. Unlike the previous four attempts, this time Joseph was allowed by God and the angel to finally take possession of the gold plates.

Joseph knew firsthand how incredibly tempting this sacred treasure was to the avaricious. Four years and a half dozen angelic visitations were required before even Joseph could prepare himself spiritually enough to take possession of them. As he took the plates from their carefully prepared hiding place, the angel starkly warned him again. Joseph explained, "The same heavenly messenger delivered them up to me with this charge: that I should be responsible for them; that if I should let them go carelessly, or through any neglect of mine, I should be cut off; but that if I would use all my endeavors to preserve them, until he, the messenger, should call for them, they should be protected."[8] Lucy Smith later recalled that Joseph explained the angel's charge in this way:

LET'S TALK ABOUT THE BOOK OF MORMON

The Palmyra—Hill Cumorah Monument, featuring the angel Moroni, was erected by the Church near where Joseph was given the gold plates.

Now you have got the Record into your own hands, and you are but a man, therefore, you will have to be watchful, and faithful to your trust or you will be overpowered by wicked men; for they will lay every plan and scheme that is possible to get them away from you; and, if you do not take heed, continually, they will succeed.— While they were in my hands, I could keep them, and no man had power to take them away; but now I give them up to you: beware and look well to your ways, and you shall have power to retain them until the time for them to be translated.[9]

This promise of divine protection was almost immediately put to the test. Fearful that he might have been followed, Joseph did not bring the plates home with him after he first obtained them, but rather hid them in an old, decaying log.

MARRYING EMMA AND OBTAINING THE PLATES

When he went to retrieve the plates from this hiding spot and finally bring them home, he decided to travel much of the way back through the woods, rather than the road, to lessen the chance of being seen with plates. Despite this careful plan, conspirators lay in wait for him.

According to Lucy Smith's version of events, as Joseph approached an area with multiple downed trees, a man wielding a gun suddenly sprang up from behind one of the logs and attacked him, clubbing Joseph with the rifle. Fueled by adrenaline, fear, and no doubt divine power, Joseph returned the blow, knocking the perpetrator down. Clutching the plates, Joseph ran through the trees to escape. But his assailants had anticipated this reaction, and soon after another hidden man lunged at Joseph. Again, Joseph struck the man hard enough that he went sprawling to the ground. In a state of near panic, Joseph continued to flee home, only to be assaulted a third time. This time, Joseph punched his attacker so violently that his thumb was either dislocated or broken. We do not know how much damage Joseph inflicted on his enemy, but the man's attack ended after he suffered Joseph's blow.[10]

Having dropped this final attacker, Joseph finally made his exhausted and terrified way to his parents' home, still lugging the plates. The transformation of Joseph's character was on full display. Years earlier, Joseph had contemplated using the plates to gain earthly wealth and fame. Now he collapsed into a chair with his dislodged thumb, having risked his life to protect the plates from those who wanted them for the same earthly value that had once tempted him. Joseph's run home with the plates was a portent of things to come. He would continually face disappointments, problems, and struggles as the Lord used him to translate the gold plates and restore His Church. In the face of those difficulties, Joseph would remain resolute and determined to fulfill God's will.

It had taken Joseph Smith most of the decade to progress from a young teenager who had humbly petitioned God to know the truth about salvation to a married man ready to undertake the marvelous translation of the gold plates and produce the published Book of Mormon. This miracle would usher in the Restoration of the gospel and powerfully impact the faith of millions of people across the world.

CHAPTER 3

EARLY TRANSLATION WITH EMMA AND MARTIN, 1828

After spending much of their first year of marriage in Palmyra, Joseph and Emma decided to move back to her parents' settlement in Harmony, Pennsylvania. It is unclear precisely what led to the decision to move; however, the months after Joseph received the plates were filled with growing antagonism from local residents and agitators. Several armed attempts were made to steal the plates and threatened the Smith family.[1]

Economic considerations also probably factored in the poor, young couple's decision. The Smith family generally had struggled to stay afloat financially since they arrived in Palmyra in 1818, necessitating more than one move since their arrival.[2] Joseph and Emma had brought nothing with them when they moved in the with Joseph's family, and now both would be unable to contribute much to the financial well-being of the Smith farm because of the sacred translation work they were to be anxiously engaged in. According to Emma's father, Isaac Hale, his daughter had written him a letter asking if her property she had left in Harmony was still there, "consisting of clothing, furniture, cows," and more. Emma likely feared that, having rejected her father's wishes by marrying Joseph, all that had been nominally hers in Harmony had been punitively confiscated by her father. Isaac Hale responded that "her property was safe and at her disposal," extending an olive branch that suggested his hurt feelings could be assuaged. The couple determined to move back to Harmony, and Emma's brother came up to Palmyra to help them move what little belongings they possessed.³ In addition, as Joseph later explained, "In the midst of our afflictions we found a friend in a Gentleman . . . Martin Harris, who came to us and gave me fifty dollars."⁴ The money helped Joseph settle his outstanding debts before the move.

But even as they escaped the dangerous situation in Palmyra for the uncomfortable reunion awaiting in Harmony, Joseph and Emma had to avoid further attempted violence. According to Lucy Smith, as the couple prepared to leave town, with the plates hidden at the bottom of a barrel of beans for safety, a mob assembled, and "their object was to follow Joe Smith and take his Gold Bible away from him." Thankfully, a family friend refused to participate in the violence, and the subsequent infighting among the mobbers allowed Joseph and Emma to escape.⁵

Moving into a separate home on Isaac Hale's property, Joseph and Emma finally had a place of their own, apparently safe from the violence that had continually threatened them in Palmyra. Their home in Harmony was a perfect place to focus on the translation of the gold plates. Though Joseph had briefly begun examining and copying some of the characters on the plates in Palmyra, after they arrived in Harmony, he "immediately . . . commenced copying the characters of all the plates."⁶ He continued to copy the characters and engaged in translating in December 1827 and January 1828. Joseph later recalled that he "copied a considerable number of" the characters.⁷ Joseph Knight Sr. and Lucy Mack Smith both remembered this period of translation to be far more than a brief examination of the plates, but rather a time when Joseph was creating an entire "alphabet" from the characters on them.⁸

Without seeing the plates themselves, Emma and her brother helped Joseph copy these characters, duplicating the images Joseph had first drawn from the plates. As Joseph

EARLY TRANSLATION WITH EMMA AND MARTIN, 1828

handed her his initial copies, Emma "drew off the characters exactly like the ancient."[9]

While Joseph and Emma were engaged in this examination of the characters, Martin Harris arrived from Palmyra. Joseph explained that Martin had come because of a powerful manifestation he had experienced: "The Lord appeared unto him in a vision and shewed unto him his marvelous work which he was about to do and he immediately came to Susquehanna and said the Lord had shown him that he must go to New York City with some of the characters." According to Joseph's later history, before Martin had arrived on this mission from God, Joseph had translated a few of the characters by the "means of the Urim and Thummim."[10] After this brief translation period, Martin Harris made a trip to New York City with transcripts of some of the characters and some of Joseph's translations. Martin may have first gone to the former Palmyra local Luther Bradish in Albany but eventually ended up presenting the documents to the renowned scholar Samuel L. Mitchill, who further directed Martin to Charles Anthon, of Columbia College.[11]

Martin showed Anthon characters from the plates "which were not yet translated, and he [Anthon] said they were Egyptian, Chaldeak, Assyriac, and Arabic."[12] Echoing Isaiah 29:11–12, Joseph Smith explained in his earliest history that Martin had taken "his Journy to the Eastern Cittys and the Learned saying read this I pray thee and the learned said I cannot but if he would bring the plates they would read it but the Lord had forbid it and he returned to me and gave them to me to translate." Joseph explained that he could not translate them because he was "not learned but he [God] had prepared spectacles for to read the Book." Joseph states that he then "commenced translating the characters and thus the Propicy of Isiaah was fulfilled with [which] is written in the 29 chaptr concerning the book."[13]

Emma Smith and Translating with the Urim and Thummim

From December 1827 to January 1828, Joseph, with Emma as his primary help, copied characters from the plates and possibly organized them into an alphabet. Emma had to take on this huge responsibility because Joseph "had no one to write [for] him but his wife." She then served as Joseph's first scribe of the miraculous translation. They continued this task "a little . . . through the winter."[14] "Day after day," Joseph dictated from the Urim and Thummim, which was placed in the bottom of his top hat to block the ambient light of the day, providing him a clear look at the device. As he dictated, Emma sat "close by him." Working in such close proximity and knowing her husband's literary abilities firsthand, Emma was amazed that he could dictate the text without a book or preprepared manuscript in front of him. According to her, he read the text out loud while looking into his hat. Emma witnessed this unlikely event over the next days and months, astonished by the miraculous nature of Joseph's dictation.

Emma explained that though there was nothing separating her and Joseph, she did not see the plates, which sat on the table. They were covered with a linen cloth, obscuring them from her view and the view of others. Still, Emma could see the shape of an actual object, heavily resting on her table. Though she never removed the covering to look directly at the plates, she did physically interact with them multiple times. She was able to feel them, "tracing their outline and shape" with her fingers through the cloth. Her touch revealed that they seemed "to be pliable like thick paper and would rustle with a metallic sound when the edges were moved." She ran her thumb down the corners of the plates, like a book, and like any other real object in the house, she "moved them from place to place" to get them out of the way of her day-to-day tasks. For Emma, the plates were absolutely a physical reality. Even covered, they were a testament that Joseph had a divine

EARLY TRANSLATION WITH EMMA AND MARTIN, 1828

mission from God. At the same time, Emma had another great witness. She continued to serve as a scribe of the translation. Emma was convinced that the words Joseph dictated to her were in fact "the word of God."[15]

Emma Smith was the first to help Joseph in translating the gold plates. She helped copy characters and prepare an alphabet, and she recorded a portion (possibly two-thirds) of the translation of the book of Lehi.

Because 116 pages of the original manuscript of the translation (often referred to as the book of Lehi) were stolen, we cannot examine the manuscript's handwriting and thus it is impossible to say with any certainty just which persons in those early days wrote for Joseph, how much they wrote, and how often. Nevertheless, available evidence suggests that Emma was likely the primary scribe for that portion of the translation: She was his scribe when he began copying characters from the gold plates and was also the first to participate in Joseph's dictation of the translation (from December to January). Because Joseph had removed to Harmony by the time the translation began in earnest, Martin Harris's service as scribe could only occur sporadically, when he was able to make the long journey down to Pennsylvania. While Martin was gone, Emma apparently acted as a scribe for the first portion of (the now lost) translation. She did not differentiate between her initial work and the work that Martin Harris would do later that spring as a scribe, making the division of labor hard to identify.[16] Though Martin clearly took part in the scribal work, he later downplayed his role by stating that "there were not many pages translated while he wrote."[17] Martin estimated that he wrote "about one third of the first part of the translation."[18] This means that he may have recorded only one-third of the book of Lehi, likely leaving the other two-thirds for Emma to record.

In any case, the founding first lady was not a minor cog in the production of the Book of Mormon. Indeed, Joseph was not able to obtain the plates until Emma supported him, and she was the first to help him in the process of learning to translate the work. Of course, Emma's involvement became more difficult when the couple expected their first child. As she neared the last months of her pregnancy, Martin's help likely became necessary.

Martin's Conviction and Lucy's Opposition

As the potential financier of the production of the Book of Mormon, Martin Harris played a significant role too. Following the commandment Martin had received from the Lord, Joseph entrusted Martin with copies of the characters drawn from the gold plates. Martin's trip to the East was a substantial risk for Joseph. What if Martin absconded with the manuscripts or became deeply at odds with the project after consulting with scholars? The innate risk in Martin's trip exhibited itself early on, when he approached John Clark, who was an Episcopal preacher in Palmyra. Clark reflected back upon the encounter and scoffed at Martin's lack of long-term devotion to one congregation, mentioning that he was once a Methodist and even embraced Universalism at one point.[19]

Clark pejoratively remembered Martin "to be floating upon the sea of uncertainty." Seeing the characters from the gold plates gave him pause, but Clark still viewed the entire project with skepticism. Martin's marriage had already been incredibly strained by his acceptance of Joseph Smith's claims. Now, Martin's reputation and honor, incredibly valuable traits in nineteenth-century America, were also being challenged by his association with Joseph Smith and the gold plates.

Despite such negative responses from those he told of the gold plates, when Martin returned, he was even more determined to pursue translation. The character transcripts themselves were evidence of the truthfulness of the work and clearly motivated Martin Harris to continue supporting Joseph. While Joseph was delighted, Lucy Harris, Martin's wife, increased her opposition to her husband's involvement. Martin was apparently somewhat estranged from Lucy prior to his involvement with Joseph but maintained a close enough relationship with her that she wanted to travel with him on his trip to visit scholars in the East. Martin had refused to allow her to accompany him, and his subsequent eagerness to fund the translation upon his return infuriated Lucy even more.[20] From those scholars, Martin had apparently received some confirmation of the authenticity of the characters and even some assurance of their accurate translation by Joseph Smith.

Desperate to derail Martin's faith in Joseph, Lucy took drastic measures. According to Lucy Mack Smith, Lucy Harris conspired with a young man name Flanders Dyke, who was courting Harris's daughter, "to get the Egyptian characters out of Martin's possession and hire a room in Palmira & transcribe them accurately."[21] Lucy Harris promised Dyke that once he had brought the transcript to her, she would allow him to marry her daughter. If true, such a long-term, life-altering promise reflects the depth of Lucy's determination to derail her husband's interest in the gold plates. Dyke indeed married her daughter and namesake, Lucy Harris, in 1828.[22]

Hopeful that Lucy could yet be convinced, Martin

encouraged her to go with him to Harmony for a few weeks to talk with Joseph. While traveling to Pennsylvania, however, it was clear that she was determined to undermine Martin and the project of translation. When Martin "exhibited the Egyptian characters" copied from the gold plates to fellow travelers in order to provide proof of Joseph Smith's claims, Lucy contrarily "took out of her pocket an exact copy of them" that had been transcribed by Flanders Dyke, preventing Martin from purveying the information in only a positive light. Satisfied that her purloined copy was succeeding in undermining Martin's testimony of the plates, "she pursued this course wherever she went until she reached" Harmony.

Once the Harrises arrived, Lucy was adamant that "she had come to see the plates" and would not return home until she had fully examined them with her own eyes. Her singular desire even breeched the sanctity of Emma's domestic affairs as Lucy rummaged through the Smiths' house in an attempt to find where the plates were hidden. Under the command of God to show no one the plates, Joseph took the plates in their box and secretly buried them. The next morning, Lucy spent most of the day searching the property for the plates. Highly disturbed, she returned to the house before taking up lodging at a neighbor's house with a story of a "tremendous great black snake" that had emerged from the property, "hissing" at her after she had disturbed its resting place. Failing to find the plates, she "continued her operations while she remained in Harmony doing all that her ingenuity could contrive to injure Joseph." She tried to convince as many people as possible that he was a "grand imposter." Then after two weeks, she returned to Palmyra with Martin and continued her tirade against Joseph, claiming that he was "robbing her husband."[23]

Martin Harris and Translation

Despite his wife's determined opposition, Martin Harris returned to Harmony again to help Joseph Smith translate the plates, this time prudently without Lucy. Emma was in the last trimester of pregnancy, and Martin's help with the translation likely relieved Emma of that additional burden. From mid-April to mid-June 1828, Martin stayed with the Smiths and served as the primary scribe, marveling as Emma had at the miraculous way in which Joseph dictated the translation.[24] Having been associated with Joseph and the plates since the fall of 1827, Martin was both thrilled and astonished by the contents of the translation. He declared, "Joseph knew not the contents of the Book of Mormon until it was translated."[25] Emma expressed similar amazement. She explained that Joseph would actually ask her questions about the text he had just dictated to her, such as whether or not walls indeed surrounded Jerusalem. Though the Book of Mormon narrative came from his own mouth, Joseph seemed to not fully comprehend everything he was speaking as he translated. Martin explained the process, stating that by the "aid of the seer stone, sentences would appear and were read by the Prophet and written" by him and Emma. Emphasizing the importance of accuracy and that it was God who determined the words of the translation, Martin explained that the words Joseph read from the seer stone would not disappear until they had been recorded correctly.[26]

By the middle of June, though the translation was not close to being finished, Martin wanted to return to Palmyra. Martin and Emma had recorded a large manuscript, which Joseph said was taken from the "Book of Lehi" recorded on the gold plates, "which was an account abridged from the plates of Lehi, by the hand of Mormon."[27] Martin explained that the book of Lehi was around one-third the size of what was published in the 1830 Book of Mormon. In the preface of the 1830 Book of Mormon, Joseph explained how "116 pages" had been stolen from him and that nomenclature became the popular way to describe this lost book of Lehi.[28]

Still desperate to convince his wife, relatives, and friends that the gold plates were real and that the translation of them was a miracle from God, Martin "began to tease [Joseph] to give him liberty to carry the writings home" to show them to his family and friends.[29] Though the characters drawn from the plates had failed to win over any converts to his side, Harris believed that, confronted with the lengthy manuscript itself, doubting loved ones would not be able to so casually dismiss Joseph Smith as a fraud.

Reluctant, but empathetic to his patron's dilemma at home, Joseph told Martin that he would ask God "through the Urim and Thummim." Joseph did as he was asked but received the disappointing answer no. He tried again, but "the answer was as before," a negative one.[30]

Joseph was in a terrible position. At this point, in the summer of 1828, virtually everyone outside of Joseph's own family had completely rejected him and his assertion that he had seen an angel and obtained gold plates. Joseph had been told by the angel that he would be the means whereby the book would be published to the world. Yet the cost of such an undertaking was utterly beyond Joseph Smith's financial capabilities. Joseph had purchased his Harmony farm from his father-in-law for two hundred dollars, which he did not have. In fact, because he could not make the payments, Isaac Hale apparently threatened to evict his own daughter and her husband. As Joseph recalled the dire situation only a few years later, "We had become reduced in property and my wives father was about to turn me out of doores & I had not where to go and I cried unto the Lord that he would provide for me to accomplish the work whereunto he had commanded me."[31] The cost of printing the Book of Mormon would be three thousand dollars, or fifteen times Joseph's entire net worth, even if he had owned his farm outright, which he did not. If Martin Harris became discouraged enough by the incessant taunting of friends and family or Lucy's constant machinations to undermine the translation project, Joseph would not only lose one of the few friends who believed him but seemingly the only person capable and willing to pay to publish the finished book.

With these circumstances weighing heavily on his mind,

and after "much solicitation" from Martin, Joseph asked God a third time to grant Martin's request. This time the request was granted. Martin was given the privilege to take the manuscript back to Palmyra but only under very specific and strict conditions. He could show the manuscript to only six named family members and no one else. Joseph "required of him that he should bind himself in a covenant" with him.[32] Harris readily agreed and fatefully set off with the manuscript back to Palmyra. It would never be seen by Joseph or Emma again.

Timeline of the Translation of The Book of Mormon

Timeframe	Assistant/Scribe	Duties	Outcome
December 1827 to January 1828	Emma Smith	Prepared characters and an alphabet; recorded the translation of some of the copied characters as scribe	Possible list of known characters on the plates; translation of some characters from the plates with Urim and Thummim
Mid-February to April 1828	Emma Smith	Recorded the translation of the lost manuscript "day after day" as scribe	Possibly two-thirds of the book of Lehi
Mid-February to March 1828	Martin Harris	Secured a secular examination of the characters	Charles Anthon's evaluation
Mid-April to mid-June 1828	Martin Harris	Continued translation of the lost manuscript	Possibly one-third of the book of Lehi
September 1828	Emma Smith	Scribe briefly to translation	Unknown
February 1829	Samuel Smith	Scribe briefly to translation	Unknown
March 1829	Martin Harris	Scribe briefly to translation	Unknown
Mid-April 1829	Oliver Cowdery	Given gift to translate like Joseph	Unsuccessful translation
April 5 to June 28, 1829	Oliver Cowdery	Scribe to translation	Nearly all of what would become the printed 1830 Book of Mormon
June 1829	John Whitmer	Scribe to translation	Translation of small sections of the small plates

CHAPTER 4

LOSS PRECEDES THE MIRACLE

Although Martin Harris had covenanted with God and Joseph that he would not show anyone the pages of the translation outside of the specified six family members, Martin found that the temptation to show it to others was just too great. As a well-respected community leader, Martin had borne the slights and taunts and whisperings of those who thought him to be utterly deluded and hoodwinked by Smith. With these pages, Martin believed, he had the proof to silence his critics and perhaps even persuade some to believe. And so, despite his covenant, Harris showed the pages to numerous inquirers. Neither of his hoped-for outcomes came to fruition.[1]

Instead, the precious pages that Joseph, Emma, and Martin had so painstakingly labored over disappeared. Frantic searches and inquiries turned up nothing, and Martin was left with the terrible prospect of reporting this colossal failure to Joseph Smith.

The pages were not stolen for monetary reasons. Though those pages would be worth millions today, they were worth nothing in 1828. Neither Joseph nor Martin was ever blackmailed with demands for a handsome cash payment for the return of the pages. However, just as Lucy Harris had manipulated the document that contained the characters from the gold plates, the book of Lehi manuscript could be used by those trying to undercut the miraculous nature of Joseph's translation of the Book of Mormon. Joseph was told precisely what the evil scheme entailed in a revelation from God. The Lord declared, "Satan hath put it into their hearts to alter the words which you . . . have translated, which have gone out of your hands. . . . Because they have altered the words, they read contrary from that which you translated . . . ; and, on this wise, the devil has sought to lay a cunning plan, that he may destroy this work; for he hath put into their hearts to do this, that by lying they may say they have caught you in the words which you have pretended to translate" (Doctrine and Covenants 10:10–13).

Joseph would later inform his readers of the theft of the pages and the calculated plan to destroy him in the preface to the Book of Mormon: "Some person or persons have stolen it . . . and if I should bring forth the same words again, or, in other words, if I should translate the same over again, they would publish that which they had stolen, and Satan would stir up the hearts of this generation, that they might not receive this work: but behold, the Lord said unto me, I will not suffer that Satan shall accomplish his evil design in this thing."[2]

Still in Harmony, Joseph did not know that the manuscript had been stolen in Palmyra, but he knew his incessant inquiries had in some way incurred the displeasure of God since the interpreters (and possibly also the plates themselves) were taken from Joseph by the same angel who had once delivered them to him. Despite this, the loss of the interpreters and Martin's extended absence with the pages were not the most pressing things on Joseph's mind. Just after Martin left, Emma gave birth to a child that was either stillborn or died immediately after birth. Emma suffered excruciating pain in the delivery and apparently nearly died due to complications from childbirth, a common cause of death for young women in the nineteenth century. On top of her physical struggles, Emma and Joseph had to endure the trauma of burying their first child.

Emma lay stricken both emotionally and physically, with Joseph at her side for weeks. Her fate was "so uncertain" that Joseph "never slept one hour in undisturbed quiet" for two weeks until she became well enough that they were not worried about the possibility of her dying.[3] Once Emma had gained some of her strength again, she told Joseph, "I cannot rest and shall not be at ease until I know something about what Mr. Harris is doing with" the manuscript.[4] Emma had spent months working on the translation. She was personally invested in the safety of those words she had so painstakingly written as Joseph dictated them. She encouraged Joseph to go to Palmyra, regardless of their dire situation at home. They had just lost a child, and Emma had nearly lost her own life, yet she wanted to know that the manuscript was still securely in Martin's possession. Conflicted, Joseph spent several excruciating days on a coach ride contemplating the death of his child and worrying about leaving his spouse in such a weak condition.

Though Martin had agreed to come to breakfast the morning after Joseph arrived in Palmyra, the early hours passed by with no sign of him. When he finally did arrive, rather than entering the house, he sat on the fence outside with his hat drawn over his eyes. All of the Smiths knew that something was wrong, but they did not know the extent of the disaster. Finally coming inside, Martin replied to the inquiry about the pages by crying out, "Oh, I have lost my soul! I have lost my soul!" Having feared something had befallen the sacred manuscript all throughout the night and into the morning, Joseph manifested his anger and frustration over his own recent difficulties. He sprang from his chair and interrogated Martin: "Have you broken your oath, and brought down condemnation upon my head, as well as your own?"[5] The family then sobbed together as they mourned the death of Emma's child, her near death, and now Martin's loss of the manuscript. After a devastating visit with his family and with little hope in the future, Joseph left the next morning to inform Emma that the translated pages were gone. He and his family "parted with heavy hearts," Lucy Mack Smith later wrote, "for it seemed as though all our fond anticipations which we had fed upon and which had been the source of so much secret gratification to all was in that moment fled and fled forever."[6]

It is important for modern Latter-day Saints to understand that Joseph and Martin were not being hyperbolic when they exclaimed that their souls were lost. The truths about the multiple kingdoms of glory, the premortal life, the eventual end to the suffering of the wicked, and the expansiveness of God's love for us and willingness to forgive had not yet been revealed to Joseph Smith. Later, powerful revelations and visions would make these things plain. But in the summer of 1828, after they had struggled for the better part of a decade to fulfill the commandments of God, only to have lost nearly the entirety of the sacred translation, the condemnation of God loomed large and permanent.

Joseph returned to Harmony a broken, hopeless man. He had lost his son, the sacred translation manuscript was gone, the interpreters had been taken away by the angel, his father-in-law still refused to accept that Joseph had been visited by angels, and his dear, still-recovering wife now had to learn that all of her efforts in writing the translation had been in vain. Indeed, perhaps all of their sacrifices had been for nothing since Joseph had brought condemnation down upon his soul. Though Joseph would experience many more trials in his life, it is hard to imagine that any of those future days seemed quite as dark as those in the summer of 1828.

Stricken with guilt and sorrow, he walked out "a little distance" from his Harmony home shortly after returning from Palmyra and was surprised as the angel Moroni appeared to him again.[7] The angel handed him the Urim and Thummim, which he had previously taken. Joseph inquired of God through the Urim and Thummim again. It was not the text of the Book of Mormon he saw this time, but a revelation from God that declared boldly that "the works, and the designs and the purposes of God, cannot be frustrated" (Doctrine and Covenants 3:1). The revelation was initially stern and harsh, declaring that Joseph "had sinned in delivering the manuscript into the hands of a wicked man," but it also soothed Joseph's troubled soul, telling him, "Remember, God is merciful" (Doctrine and Covenants 3:10). Joseph had twice before in his life felt like he was under divine condemnation for his sins, and in each case his earnest prayers had resulted in heavenly visions and the assurance that his sins were forgiven. If he would repent, the divine revelation told him, "Thou art still chosen."[8] He explained that after receiving this revelation, "both the plates, and the Urim and Thummim were taken from me again, but in a few days they were returned to me."[9]

Back in Palmyra, Lucy and Joseph Smith Sr. could no longer bear to wait for Joseph to return. Having last seen their son devastated and depressed at the loss of the pages and his child, they proactively determined they would go to Harmony to visit and comfort Joseph and Emma. Joseph saw them approach from a distance, and Lucy remembered that Joseph "met us with a countenance blazing with delight and it was very evident that his joy did not arise wholly from seeing us."[10] Emma was not on her deathbed, and the plates were back in Joseph's possession. In fact, Lucy remembered that the plates were carefully stored in a Moroccan trunk in Emma's bureau. Emma's life had been preserved, and Joseph had a renewed interest in the translation of the plates. Before too long, Emma began recording the translation for Joseph, though the angel "said that the Lord would send some one to write for him."[11] Emma was always eager to be involved, but they did not return earnestly to the translation until April 1829. And after they returned home, Lucy and Joseph Sr. would help turn the next page in the story of the translation.

Transitioning Back to the Translation

The bustling town of Palmyra was still telling the story of the gold plates and Joseph Smith. The Erie Canal brought travelers and traders to its city center daily, drawing farmers in from Canandaigua and the Finger Lakes who bought and sold goods transported on the interior waterway. The sincere curiosity of Palmyra residents about the plates and translation provoked deep interest in the entire Smith family. The accounts of witnesses who had held and heard the metal plates in the box, coupled with the circulating copies of ancient characters and the scandal of the missing manuscript pages, proved to be an intriguing source of rumor in the surrounding areas.

In the fall of 1828, one important visitor heard the stories of the gold plates, and it changed the entire trajectory of his life, whom he would marry, and what his religious convictions would be. His name was Oliver Cowdery. Born in Wells, Vermont, Oliver had traveled to Palmyra seeking work. His older brother Lyman had just recently been offered a teaching job in Palmyra but had better offers elsewhere, so Oliver "requested them to receive him in [Lyman's] place." Needing a place to stay, Oliver "requested [Joseph Smith Sr.] to take him as a boarder at least for a little while until he should become acquainted with his patrons in the school."[12] At the Smith's house Oliver and Joseph Sr. inevitably talked about the gold plates and Joseph Jr.'s purported possession of them. Cowdery also heard and participated in discussions about the plates with skeptical local residents in Palmyra. Cowdery's interest would eventually materialize in the largest production of text of the entire translation project.

Despite the local gossip and skepticism, some inquirers became convinced of the veracity of the Book of Mormon translation during this period. In early 1829, Joseph indicated to his family that he would begin translating again. Joseph Sr. and his son Samuel traveled to Harmony to stay with Joseph and Emma, but they stopped first in Colesville to visit Joseph Knight Sr. As a longtime family friend, Knight was apparently convinced by what the travelers had to say about the gold plates and became eager to help. In the dead of winter he insisted that he "would go with [his] sleigh and take them down" to Harmony. Joseph Knight talked with the Smiths for hours through the night and left them with money to support their travel and the cost of paper and ink to begin the translation of the Book of Mormon again.[13] Joseph started to translate with

Emma, and he even briefly employed his brother Samuel as a scribe, but Joseph had to return to some of his farm work that fall, so it seems little progress was made.[14]

Before his family left, Joseph delivered a revelation from God to his father, encouraging him that the "field is white already to harvest" (Doctrine and Covenants 4:4) and that he should reap the crops by preparing the world for Christ's triumphal Second Coming. As Joseph worked hard in the soil, found comfort in a visit from his family, and received encouragement from on high through revelation, momentum was building to start the translation in earnest again.

Martin's Desire to See the Plates

Once Joseph Sr. and Samuel returned home, the revelation and their enthusiasm for the translation was contagious to both Martin and Oliver. Unfortunately, when Martin got excited again, so did his wife, Lucy. The gold plates were a popular topic in town, and Lucy apparently talked to every person she could to build a case against the reality of the plates. She searched for witnesses who would undermine Joseph and Martin's claims about the plates. Though there was not an official trial, witnesses were gathered to present a case against Joseph for fraud. Martin recalled that "in March [1829] the people rose up and united against the work, gathering testimony against the Plates and said they had testimony enough and if I did not put Joseph in jail and his father for deception they would [arrest] me."[15]

People had witnessed the box that Joseph kept the plates in, and some had even tried to steal the plates, but no one had actually seen the plates outright. To prove their case, the detractors needed to identify the object inside the box. One asserted that it was sand, another claimed it was a large rock, and a more believable witness claimed the object was metal but not an ancient set of gold plates. Though it is clear that many in Palmyra took it as foregone conclusion that the plates were real and in Joseph's possession and thus tried to steal them, even those who believed Joseph had not yet seen the plates. Making things worse, Lucy Harris had hefted the box the plates were in and heard the contents inside but had determined it all to be a fraud, since she had never actually seen the plates. To Lucy Harris and likeminded Palmyrans, the plates must have been a fraud or Joseph would have simply shown them to everyone.[16]

Those who did not believe the gold plates were real could not be convinced otherwise without a direct examination of the plates; nonetheless, Martin Harris and others insisted that they were real as a matter of faith. Their participation in the production of a translation manuscript was based on much more than just the weight and sound of the plates in the box. Fearing the threats of criminal and civil action against himself and the Smiths levied by his wife and others, Martin set out for Harmony to convince Joseph to allow him to finally see the plates. Lucy, on the other hand, plotted to uncover the fraud by sending a man named "Mr. Rogers" with Martin. They got on the coach together and spoke of the plates. Rogers had planned to tear the cover off the plates or break open the box to see what was inside, but his nefarious plan failed when, for unknown reasons, he didn't actually make it to Harmony with Martin.[17]

When Martin arrived in February 1829 with hopes to assure the world of the reality of the plates, he was surprised to learn that Joseph also wanted Harris to see the plates, despite the terrible experiences regarding the lost manuscript the summer previous. But Joseph would not again let his desire to mitigate antagonists and assuage Martin's feelings tempt him to pressure the Lord beyond a single inquiry into the matter. At this point, Joseph had kept the plates hidden from every other person in the world, including his own wife, for a year and a half. He had promised God he would not show them, and therefore only God could grant Martin permission to view the plates. After Martin's inquiry, Joseph took the box with the plates, without revealing them to Martin, to the nearby woods to bury them in the ground. He then turned it over to God to decide whether it was time for Martin to see them. Martin followed Joseph's footprints to the burial spot but could find no plates.

Joseph then decided to ask God directly through the Urim and Thummim.[18] The revelation Joseph received promised Martin that if he were faithful, he would be shown the plates eventually, but not at that moment. The revelation also testified of the truthfulness of the text that was being produced through the translation process (see Doctrine and Covenants 5). The translated text would enlighten the world and reveal an ancient American past to the modern reader. The book of Lehi should have been enough to demonstrate the miracle of translation and allow Martin to trust that the plates were real. Indeed, the revelation provided commentary on the skepticism and faithlessness of humankind: "Behold, if they will not believe my words, they would not believe you, my servant Joseph, if it were possible that you should show them all these things which I have committed unto you" (Doctrine and Covenants 5:7). There would never be enough evidence to appease those who sought a sign as a basis for their conversion. If a person could not, through the Spirit, read the words of the translation and the words of that very revelation and discern that they were the words of God, they would not believe even if the plates were laid bare on the table in front of them.

Martin himself had received numerous witnesses of the divinity of the work. By early 1829, he had (1) carefully interviewed the Smith family in 1827, searching for cracks in their stories; (2) seen a vision from God commanding him to pay for the publication of the Book of Mormon that fall; (3) traveled across the country allowing scholars to examine the gold-plate characters in the winter of 1828; (4) helped translate the lost manuscript in the spring of 1828; (5) and again, in the winter of 1829, participated in the miraculous translation and received a revelation from God in answer to a question. Martin returned to Palmyra without having seen the plates themselves, with only the promise that he would see them one day if he remained faithful.

Oliver Cowdery's Arrival

Back in Palmyra, Oliver Cowdery was doing his own investigation of Joseph Smith and the gold plates. When Cowdery's friend David Whitmer first heard about the gold plates, he wondered whether Joseph really possessed them. At one point, he spoke with Oliver Cowdery in Palmyra about the rumor. Oliver offered important insights into the dilemma and sent David away hoping that it was true. There were also social and physical clues that could provide assurance that the plates were real. A handful of people had hefted the plates, and a few people had written the words of the translation. Beyond these direct witnesses, local money diggers had searched the hill where Joseph had found the plates. There they discovered exactly what they would have expected to find if Joseph had dug up an ancient set of plates: there was a large hole near the top of the hill that had recently been excavated. For decades, the rocks that presumably had held the plates in place were rumored to be on the hill, even after the hill had been plowed.[19]

Like Martin Harris's experience, the evidence Oliver compiled was not all social and physical but also spiritual and visionary. Before he had even met Joseph Smith, the "Lord appeared unto . . . Oliver Cowdery and shewed unto him the plates in a vision and also the truth of the work . . . that the Lord was about to do through [Joseph] his unworthy Servant."[20] Like Martin, who'd had a similar vision, Oliver saw the Lord and the plates and was offered a witness of the truthfulness of the work and saw his divine calling to help produce the Book of Mormon. This remarkable experience drove him to travel to Harmony to make Joseph's acquaintance. He and Samuel first traveled down to Fayette to share their plans with David Whitmer, who was also now eager to get involved and support the project. In fact, David and Oliver wrote letters back and forth discussing the plates and the translation for several weeks after Oliver and Samuel had left.[21] Oliver

LOSS PRECEDES THE MIRACLE

and Samuel finally arrived in Harmony on April 5, 1829, and Oliver started serving as a scribe for Joseph's translation just two days later.

Cowdery's arrival ushered in a new era of the translation. The previous year and a half had been characterized by halting and uneven progress, coupled with the shattering loss of the manuscript they had worked so hard to produce. Now, Cowdery and Joseph would be able to have a singular focus, and incredible progress would be made in the space of a few short weeks.

CHAPTER 5

FINISHING THE WORK

Oliver and the Translation of the Large Plates, Mormon, Ether, and Moroni

Oliver and Joseph seemed to trust each other before they had ever met. When Oliver arrived, he helped Joseph secure a legal property agreement with Isaac Hale. Emma's father had graciously allowed Joseph and Emma to move onto a portion of Isaac's property, but Joseph had not been able to make the payments to his father-in-law on time. Hale's earlier hopes that Joseph would abandon his claim of angelic visions and gold plates had given way to a growing animosity that his love for his daughter Emma would not mitigate. Indeed, as Joseph described it, by the spring of 1829, "we had become reduced in property and my wife's father was about to turn me out of doors." Oliver may have staved off that pending eviction by donating his teacher's salary to secure the property from Hale.[1] As Emma and Martin had done before, Oliver then took up the role of scribe for the translation, and Joseph immediately began dictating the Book of Mormon text to him.[2]

As soon as they started translating, Joseph delivered a revelation to Oliver from God by means of the Urim and Thummim. Oliver watched and listened as Joseph's dictation seamlessly changed from the translation of the plates to a personal revelation. While he had no way to verify that the translation of the plates was accurate, he had every reason to believe that the revelation Joseph dictated to him was correct, since it was about him. He didn't know Egyptian, nor had he seen the plates, but he knew his own personal experiences. He wrote to David Whitmer stating that Joseph "had told him secrets of his [own] life that he knew could not be known to any person but himself, in any other way than by revelation from the Almighty."[3] The revelation declared, "Blessed art thou . . . for thou has inquired of me," speaking of his vision that had provoked his travel to Harmony. The revelation went on: "Thou hast received instruction of my Spirit," or "thou wouldst not have come to" Harmony. The revelation referenced Oliver's private vision of the Lord and the plates as a "witness," asking him once again, now that he was with Joseph, "Did I not speak peace to your mind concerning the matter?"[4] (Doctrine and Covenants 6:14, 23). It was as if Oliver and the Lord were continuing a conversation they had begun earlier. Now in Harmony, the private conversation continued as the voice of Lord fell from the lips of the prophet Joseph.

The revelation declared, "Thou hast a gift, and blessed art though because of thy gift" (Doctrine and Covenants 6:10). Explaining that gift, Oliver was told that each time he had inquired of God, he "received instruction" (Doctrine and Covenants 6:14). This too explained, to some extent, how Joseph was receiving the translation and the revelation he was dictating to Oliver: he had been given a gift and received the Lord's instruction. The relationship between the translation and the revelation was clearly apparent to Oliver since the Lord told him, "I grant unto you a gift if you desire of me, to translate even as my servant Joseph" (Doctrine and Covenants 6:25). The Lord declared, perhaps speaking literally, that with their gifts, and "where two or three are gathered together in my name, as touching one thing, behold there will I be in the midst of them." Then the Lord declared, "Even so am I in the midst of you" (Doctrine and Covenants 6:32).[5] This declaration suggests that there could have been another vision, perhaps seen through the Urim and Thummim, or perhaps the Lord was actually in their midst. Either way, the Lord was there, and Oliver was learning how Joseph was dictating the translation of the Book of Mormon.

As with the revelation to Oliver and Joseph's previous translations, it was God who delivered the words of the Book of Mormon to him. This implies that Joseph had not identified which words of the translation corresponded to the characters on the gold plates. Joseph and Oliver trusted that God would guide them through the translation, and so they began recording the story of King Benjamin in the book of Mosiah. They moved quickly for several weeks, writing down scripture that covered several hundred years of history. Within the first few weeks of translation, Oliver recorded the story of King Limhi, who had also possessed gold plates "filled with engravings" that he could not translate. A missionary named Ammon took the gold plates to King Mosiah, who had "[interpreters] wherewith that he can look, and translate all records that are of ancient date; and it is a gift from God." He had "things . . . called interpreters" through which a chosen individual of God, called a seer, could see the translation of ancient characters (Mosiah 8:13). As Oliver recorded Joseph's dictation and as Joseph looked into the Urim and Thummim, they recorded, "Ammon said that a seer is a revelator and a prophet also; and a gift which is greater can no man have, except he should possess the power of God, which no man can; yet a man may have great power given him from God" (Mosiah 8:16). The words Joseph received about King Mosiah also described what was happening to Joseph and Oliver. They too had been chosen, and they too were translating gold plates with interpreters.

Oliver wondered too whether he was a seer. He had certainly been chosen, since Joseph's revelation told him that he had a gift to translate. As they translated, Joseph paused again to give Cowdery another revelation that encouraged him to translate. The revelation declared, "If thou wilt inquire thou shalt know mysteries that are great and marvelous" (Doctrine and Covenants 6:11). He was encouraged that God had granted him "a gift . . . to translate even as . . . Joseph" (Doctrine and Covenants 6:25). For King Mosiah and Joseph, all they apparently had to do was *look* into their interpreters and see the translation, but the revelation told Oliver that one also needed the right state of mind and heart. The revelation tried to connect with Oliver on a cultural level by comparing translation to how he would find subterranean water for a well—it was an ambiguous process that could nonetheless be done.[6] The revelation also compared translation to Moses's ability to guide Israel across the Red Sea on dry ground, emphasizing the miraculous nature of the translation. Joseph also demonstrated another piece of translation for Oliver. In answering the question of whether John had been translated, God revealed to Joseph that there was an ancient lost record of John. God identified the record and translated it with the answer that John had been "taken up by the Spirit, or buried by the hand of the Lord."[7] Despite these attempts to introduce Oliver to his gifts and enable him to use them, the window of time in which the Lord allowed it rapidly closed, and Oliver failed to translate.

Amid what seemed like Oliver's apprenticeship to translation, they worked together as partners to record God's translation of the Book of Mormon. They learned as they translated that the ancient prophet/historian Mormon had taken many records and utilized them to create a set of plates that was an abridgment of the original sources, with Mormon's commentary throughout. His abridged record began with Lehi's family in Jerusalem and related more than nine hundred years of history, prophesy, and miracles among the Nephites and Lamanites. Mormon then included his own book, explaining the downfall of the Nephite civilization before he passed the records to his son Moroni. Moroni not only completed his father's book but also added his own to the plates and inserted a far more ancient record called the book of Ether into the plates.

However, these plates were in a language that Joseph could not understand, leaving him totally reliant on the power of God for the translation. Oliver explained, "Day after day I continued, uninterrupted, to write from his [Joseph's] mouth, as he translated, with the Urim and Thummim, or, as the Nephites would have said, 'Interpreters.'"[8]

The translation evoked several spiritual experiences, but one particular part led to angelic visits from heaven. Oliver explained that "after writing the account given of the Savior's ministry to the remnant of the seed of Jacob upon this continent," Joseph stated that he saw that "none had authority from God to administer the ordinance of the gospel." Joseph and Oliver wanted to baptize each other, and the Book of Mormon demonstrated how Jesus had offered up the power to baptize (3 Nephi 11:21–23). In response to their inquiry about this authority, John the Baptist visited Joseph and Oliver to provide them the power to baptize. He then told them to baptize each other, and soon thereafter they even baptized Joseph's brother Samuel.[9]

This miraculous experience was followed by an even greater one. Peter, James, and John, Apostles of Jesus Christ, appeared to Joseph and Oliver and gave them even higher authority. The Lord explained these events in a revelation to Joseph Smith:

> John I have sent unto you, my servants, Joseph Smith, Jun,, and Oliver Cowdery, to ordain you unto the first priesthood which you have received, that you might be called and ordained even as Aaron. . . . And also with Peter, and James, and John, whom I have sent unto you, by whom I have ordained you and confirmed you to be apostles, and especial witnesses of my name, and bear the keys of your ministry and of the same things which I revealed unto them; unto whom I have committed the keys of my kingdom, and a dispensation of the gospel for the last times; and for the fulness of times, in the which I will gather together in one all things, both which are in heaven, and which are on earth." (Doctrine and Covenants 27:12–13)

In the space of only a few months, Joseph and Oliver went from wondering where the authority of God could be obtained to being ordained Apostles of the Lord under the very hands of Christ's Apostles from His ancient Church. In 2020, the First Presidency and the Council of the Twelve Apostles issued a proclamation titled "The Restoration of the Fulness of the Gospel of Jesus Christ," describing this angelic restoration of authority: "We affirm that under the direction of the Father and the Son, heavenly messengers came to instruct Joseph and reestablish the Church of Jesus Christ. The resurrected John the Baptist restored the authority to baptize by immersion for the remission of sins. Three of the original twelve Apostles—Peter, James, and John—restored the apostleship and keys of priesthood authority."[10] After Joseph received this authority, it was revealed to him the way the Church of Christ should be restored, including various offices and their responsibilities. Indeed, that revelation declared to Joseph "the precise day upon which, according to his will and commandment, [they] should proceed to organize his Church once again, here upon the earth."[11]

Joseph and Oliver were being guided along by God as the translation was revealed to them. Since the translation was coming directly from God, they seemed to have no sense of when the translation would end, until it did. Not knowing what was coming next, they would have had difficulty imagining what the overall project would eventually look like. In particular, Joseph wondered whether they would retranslate the manuscript Martin had lost. In response, the Lord revealed, "Those things that you have written [the lost manuscript] . . . are engraven upon the plates of Nephi" (Doctrine and Covenants 10:38). This revelation presented something like a table of contents, revealing to Joseph that the plates of Nephi, or the small plates, included two parts: the abridgment of Lehi's writing (the lost manuscript) and a first-person account of the same period, focusing on prophetic statements and the spiritual revelation that came during the same period. The Lord declared, "According to their faith in their prayers will I bring this part of my gospel to the knowledge of my people. Behold I do not bring it to destroy that which they have received, but to build it up" (Doctrine and Covenants 10:52).[12]

The Book of Mormon itself describes the miracle that these smaller plates were included by the prophet/historian Mormon. In order to create his book, Mormon searched through the numerous records he had available to him, summarizing the content as he felt inspired. In his resulting abridgement of the history of his people, Mormon included the events and miracles that he believed were most important. But after he had already completed his abridgment of the record down to the time of King Benjamin, he then serendipitously found another record that covered the same period. These "smaller" plates contained first-person accounts of the prophets from the period he had just completed. He explained,

> And now, I speak somewhat concerning that which I have written; for after I had made an abridgment from the plates of Nephi, down to the reign of this king Benjamin, of whom Amaleki spake, I searched among the records which had been delivered into my hands, and I found these plates, which contained this small account of the prophets, from Jacob down to the reign of this king Benjamin, and also many of the words of Nephi. And the things which are upon these plates pleasing me, because of the prophecies of the coming of Christ; . . . I shall take these plates, which contain these prophesyings and revelations, and put them with the remainder of my record, for they are choice unto me; and I know they will be choice unto my brethren. (Words of Mormon 1:3–6)

But Mormon did not decide to include the small plates he had found simply because he had missed them in his initial abridgment. He informs the reader that he had been moved upon by a higher power: "And I do this for a wise purpose; for thus it whispereth me, according to the workings of the Spirit of the Lord which is in me. And now, I do not know all things; but the Lord knoweth all things which are to come; wherefore, he worketh in me to do according to his will" (Words of Mormon 1:7). Among the many miracles of the translation process, the text declared that Mormon had been inspired more than two millennia earlier to include plates that provided an alternative to the book of Lehi, which would be stolen in the future.

The Translation Moves to Fayette and the Whitmer Farm

As Joseph and Oliver finished the final sentences of the Book of Mormon, they reached a perfect point to get more supplies and prepare for the translation of the small plates. The translation had consumed their lives day after day for around six weeks, and they had no money or time to support themselves. They searched for work to no avail, so Joseph Knight Sr. again came to their financial rescue, supplying paper and food, including ten bushels of grain, six bushels of potatoes, a pound of tea, and an entire barrel of mackerel. Finances were only part of their problem, unfortunately. Isaac Hale and the surrounding community apparently knew about the translation work at Joseph's house and strongly pressured them to stop and even threatened that a mob might attack the farm.[13]

However, Joseph was no longer wholly without friends outside of his family. Oliver turned to his friend David Whitmer, who he had eagerly corresponded with while he was in Harmony. Joseph stated that David and the Whitmer family "become our zealous friends and assistants in the work."[14] In fact, David serendipitously asked them if they wanted to stay with them in Fayette, New York, where the Whitmer family could provide for their needs and give them a quiet place to finish the translation of the Book of Mormon. The Whitmers were in the middle of crop rotation and had days and days of work before they could be ready for Joseph and Oliver to arrive. David went to work sowing the seeds of their farm, accomplishing double the work that he would have normally done. Apparently, unknown to David, there were three other men who slipped onto their property and diligently worked without pay.[15]

David diligently finished his work and rushed to Harmony to move Oliver and Joseph to Fayette. Mary Whitmer remained at home, overwhelmed like David, but eager to have them arrive and translate in her home. David felt like he was doing God's will, and when he arrived in Harmony, he packed Joseph's and Oliver's items into his wagon. Before they left, David wondered where they had put the plates because he had not seen them loaded into the wagon. Yet miles into their travels, they saw an old man walking down the road who told them that he was on his way to Cumorah, the hill mentioned in the translation, where Moroni had buried the plates. Curious, they offered him a ride in the back of the wagon. Astonished, David looked at Joseph with a startled gaze, and by the time he returned his eye to the old man again, the man had disappeared. Lucy Smith explained that the man had been assigned to carry the plates to Fayette.[16] Once the plates were securely in Fayette, the old man apparently offered Mary Whitmer a view of the gold plates. While preparing her house, she met the old man, who stated, "You have been very faithful and diligent in your labors, but you are tired because the increase of your toil, it is proper therefore that you should receive a witness that your faith may be strengthened." This miraculous experience left Mary Whitmer as the only known female witness of the gold plates. Much like Emma, this remarkable woman was eager to contribute to the translation of the Book of Mormon.[17]

Within a week after they arrived, Joseph and his friends started preparing for the publication of the Book of Mormon. They even translated the cover to make an application for the copyright of the book. As they baptized the Whitmers and others, the text of the Book of Mormon provoked questions of a church and church government. Joseph stated that "from this time forth many became believers, and were baptized, whilst we continued to instruct and persuade as many as applied for information."[18] By revelation, David was commanded to "seek to bring forth and establish Zion" (Doctrine

FINISHING THE WORK

Mary Whitmer is the only known female eyewitness of the gold plates.

and Covenants 12:6), and Oliver to seek to call twelve disciples, as Jesus had done in the Book of Mormon text.[19] John Whitmer briefly translated with Joseph, and Oliver extracted the foundations of a church government from Moroni's words. Oliver copied directly from the Book of Mormon text since one of Joseph's revelations told him to "rely upon the things which are written; for in them are all things written, concerning [the Lord's] church, [the Lord's] gospel, and [the Lord's] rock" (Doctrine and Covenants 18:3).[20] These principles that Oliver recorded became "articles" of the church that they were seeking to establish. The articles prescribed priesthood offices and gave directions regarding ordinances, like baptism and the administration of the sacrament of the Lord's Supper.[21]

The Three and Eight Witnesses

In June 1829, several families associated with the Smiths were filled with faith and hope as Joseph and Oliver brought the translation to an end, but the crowning moments came through revelation, vision, and witnesses of the gold plates. Since 1822, when Joseph was first told of the gold plates, he had been keeping a secret. He had spent four years preparing to acquire the plates, and he had possessed them for around twenty-one months (except for the time the angel took them back in June 1828). He had done everything he could to prove to his family and friends that the plates were real, including letting them heft, hear, and feel them through a cloth, without breaking his promise to keep them hidden from anyone's view. He had also translated with Emma, Martin, and Oliver for months, demonstrating the divine power associated with the plates and the text that shone forth from darkness. Finally others, including Mary Whitmer and eleven men, would now bear the burden of witnessing the plates.

Before their vision, Joseph, Oliver, David, and Martin "went into a grove a short distance from the house where they continued in earnest supplication to God until he permitted an angel from his presence to bear to them a message."[22] Martin was not ready and did not see the angel immediately. He left, knowing he was not in the right state of mind, walking deeper into the woods to find solace. Joseph explained that he, Oliver, and David "beheld a light above us in the air of exceeding brightness, and behold, an angel stood before us; in his hands he held the plates which we had been praying for these to have a view of: he turned over the leaves one by one, so that we could see them, and discern the engravings theron distinctly."[23] When the vision was finished, Joseph found Martin, and all together, they "once more beheld, and [saw], and heard the same things." Then like the others, Martin rejoiced, "Tis enough, tis enough; mine eyes have beheld, mine eyes have beheld."[24]

The experience of each witness was slightly different from the others', offering uniquely important testaments of the gold plates. In particular, Oliver Cowdery, David Whitmer, and Martin Harris were witnesses of much more than just the physical reality of the gold plates. First, each of them signed that they saw the plates, "which is a record of the people of Nephi, and also of the Lamanites, their brethren, and also the people of Jared."[25] This statement was a witness to the reality of the people described in the Book of Mormon, not just the empirical reality of the record. They were able to sign their names to the witness document not just because Moroni appeared and displayed the plates before them, but also because of the artifacts he showed them.

Revealing the ancient past through prehistoric artifacts, the angel showed them physical objects of the culture of the Nephites, Lamanites, and Jaredites. Two stones (likely different from the Urim and Thummim, which Oliver Cowdery had already seen Joseph use) were displayed before them. The Lord had delivered these stones to the brother of Jared before he and his people arrived in the Americas, and they were later used by Moroni to translate the record of his vision on the mountain. The Three Witnesses also saw the sword of Laban and the Liahona, artifacts from Lehi's journey from Jerusalem to the Americas, each of which had been passed from prophet to prophet throughout the narrative of the Book of Mormon. These items demonstrated the historical reality of events described in the Book of Mormon. David explained that he, Martin, and Oliver "not only saw the plates of the Book of Mormon but also the brass plates, the plates of the Book of Ether, the plates containing the records of the wickedness and secret combinations of the people of the world down to the time of their being engraved, and many other plates," along with the historical paraphernalia.[26]

Second, these three men signed as witnesses that the gold plates had "been translated by the gift and power of God."[27] This was far different than their first witness but equally important. Knowing that Joseph would be declared the author of the Book of Mormon, they heard God's voice testify that He was responsible for the translation. Having heard the voice from heaven, they declared, "We know of a surety that the work is true."[28] Thirdly, offering a witness both of the physical reality of the artifacts and of a miraculous angelic visitation, they signed the statement, "We declare with words of soberness, that an angel of God came down from heaven, and he brought and laid [the plates] before our eyes."[29]

Eight more witnesses were chosen from the Smith family (Joseph's brothers Hyrum and Samuel and his father, Joseph Sr.) and the Whitmer family (Christian, Jacob, Peter Jr., John, and their brother-in-law Hiram Page). Their witness was a tactile experience, based primarily on the physical senses of touch and sight. John Whitmer explained that Joseph handed him the plates "uncovered into our hands, and we turned the leaves sufficient to satisfy us." These eight individuals signed that they had witnessed the reality of the gold plates, declaring "the leaves . . . we did handle with our hands" and that they "saw the engravings thereon." John said that the plates "were very heavy . . . So far as I recollect, 8 by 6 or 7 inches . . . [the leaves were] just so thick, that characters could be engraven on both sides[and they were bound] in three rings, each one in the shape of a D."[30] The Eight Witnesses wrote, "We also saw the engravings thereon, all of which has the appearance of ancient work, and of curious workmanship."[31] Unlike the Three Witnesses, they did not feel and touch the sword of Laban or the other items, nor did God witness to them of the translation, but they did examine the plates and witness that they were authentic, without signs of fraud or modern marks. These men were not easily deceived individuals, and all of them were older than Joseph. Christian Whitmer was an active constable in Fayette, for example, and would have known better than to sign an affidavit that he was unwilling to legally support.

By the end of June, the translation was finished, and Joseph returned the plates to the angel. Though the odyssey of translation had finally come to a close, Joseph received little respite as he began the struggle to find a willing printer and, in the process, raised the ire of Jonathan Hadley, who would, unwittingly, in an attempt to defame and mock Joseph Smith, provide even more evidence for the miraculous story of Joseph Smith, the translation, and the Book of Mormon.[32]

CHAPTER 6
HOW DID JOSEPH TRANSLATE THE BOOK OF MORMON?

For many Latter-day Saints, the miraculous events and interesting stories surrounding the translation of the Book of Mormon are both well known and faith promoting. The fact that the monumental book that contains the translation of the gold plates exists at all is indeed proof of Joseph Smith's claims, and even well-regarded historians outside the faith have concluded that the Book of Mormon should "rank among the great achievements of American literature."[1]

Over three years after he finished translating most of the Book of Mormon, Joseph attempted to produce a history of the extraordinary events of his early life, including his First Vision, the visitations from Moroni, and the translation of the gold plates. Though Joseph was clearly attempting to write something powerful and clear, the portion of the manuscript in his own handwriting demonstrates, in part, the limitations of his writing abilities and education to that point: "We were deprived of the bennifit of an education suffice it to say I was mearly instructtid in reading writing and the ground rules of Arithmatic which constuted my whole literary acquirements. At about the age of twelve years my mind become seriously imprest with regard to the all importent concerns for the wellfare of my immortal Soul which led me to searching the scriptures."[2] This history is riddled with the spelling and grammatical errors one might expect from a poor young farmer/laborer with little formal education. There are likewise dozens of other examples of Joseph Smith's personal writing, years after the translation had been completed and after Joseph had

HOW DID JOSEPH TRANSLATE THE BOOK OF MORMON?

undertaken great efforts to educate himself, that seem to demonstrate that he could not produce the text of the Book of Mormon by his own skill.

Of course, neither Joseph Smith nor any of the scribes who aided him with the translation claimed the translation was a result of Joseph's writing abilities. Emma Smith reminded inquirers that Joseph "could neither write nor dictate a coherent and well-worded letter; let alone [dictate] a book like the Book of Mormon." As she served as his primary scribe in that first year of translation, Emma was continually amazed that her husband was somehow dictating a text that seemed completely beyond his educational abilities. "Though I was an active participant in the scenes that transpired," she reflected with earnestness, "and was present during the translation of the plates, and had cognizance of things as they transpired, it is marvelous to me, 'a marvel and a wonder,' as much so as to anyone else."[3]

Indeed, Joseph repeatedly affirmed that he translated the Book of Mormon "through the gift and power of God," using the stones God had prepared for just that purpose. The angel had explained that the stones had been divinely prepared "for the purpose of translating the book."[4] And, after Martin Harris returned from his unsuccessful mission to visit linguistic scholars in the eastern cities, Joseph lamented that he was not educated enough to take up the task of translation, "but the Lord had prepared spectacles for to read the Book therefore I commenced translating the characters."[5]

As we examine the process by which Joseph translated the gold plates, it may be helpful to first consider what the Book of Mormon itself has to say about translation. The angel declared to Joseph that sacred stones had been prepared and buried with the plates for the purpose of translating them, but the Book of Mormon text itself also makes multiple references to these devices and the process of translation.

One of the most memorable accounts from the Book of Mormon is the experience of the brother of Jared, who demonstrated his faith by creating stones for the Lord to touch to give light to the Jaredites as they crossed the ocean in their barges. As part of that experience, the brother of Jared was also shown many things in a vision and told to record them, even though his language would be indecipherable. And the Lord gave two stones to him for the purpose of future translation: "And behold, when ye shall come unto me, ye shall write them and shall seal them up, that no one can interpret them; for ye shall write them in a language that they cannot be read. And behold, these two stones will I give unto thee, and ye shall seal them up also with the things which ye shall write" (Ether 3:22–23).

The Lord further explained, "I will cause in my own due time that these stones shall magnify to the eyes of men these things which ye shall write" (Ether 3:24). Moroni, the prophet who abridged the book of Ether, explained that, along with the plates, he had "sealed up the interpreters, according to the commandment of the Lord" (Ether 4:5).

While the book of Ether gives the best explanation of these stones that were prepared by the Lord, the book of Mosiah gives some insight into how such miraculous translations took place. After Ammon found the people of Limhi and disabused them of the notion that he was one of the wicked priests of King Noah, King Limhi asked Ammon "if he could interpret languages" (Mosiah 8:6). Limhi explained how, in their attempts to find Zarahemla and the rest of the Nephites, his people had found a ruined civilization (that of the Jaredites) along with twenty-four gold plates with writings on them that they could not read.

After Limhi asked if he knew anyone who could translate, Ammon explained: "I can assuredly tell thee, O king, of a man that can translate the records; *for he has wherewith that he can look*, and translate all records that are of ancient date; and it is a gift from God. And the things are called interpreters, and no man can look in them except he be commanded, lest he should look for that he ought not and he should perish.

HOW DID JOSEPH TRANSLATE THE BOOK OF MORMON?

And whosoever is commanded to look in them, the same is called seer" (Mosiah 8:13; emphasis added).

Ammon's description of King Mosiah's ability to translate explained how the king interacted with these interpreters. He did not simply have them in his pocket or possession, but he looked into or through the device in order to translate. When Mosiah translated the Jaredite records, "he translated them by the means of those two stones which were fastened into the two rims of a bow" (Mosiah 28:13). Further, Mormon provided this commentary on translating with those stones: "Now these things were prepared from the beginning, and were handed down from generation to generation, for the purpose of interpreting languages; and they have been kept and preserved by the hand of the Lord, that he should discover to every creature who should possess the land the iniquities and abominations of his people; and whosoever has these things is called seer, after the manner of old times" (Mosiah 28: 13–16).

This description of the purpose and use of the stones is why these interpreters are often referred to as "seer stones." The description of the stones being "fastened into two rims of a bow" matches the description of the translation device the angel first told Joseph Smith was buried up with the plates.[6]

But the Book of Mormon also mentions a separate translation device, one apparently different from the two stones prepared for the brother of Jared or used by Mosiah in his translation of the Jaredite plates. This single stone even has a name: Gazelem. Alma referred to this stone when committing to Helaman's charge all of the records that had been handed down since the time of Nephi. When discussing how these things would be declared to the world, he revealed that "the Lord said: I will prepare unto my servant Gazelem, a stone, which shall shine forth in darkness unto light" (Alma 37:23).

Just by examining the text of the Book of Mormon and Joseph Smith's account of the angel Moroni appearing in his room, one might come to several conclusions about how the translation of the gold plates took place:

1. God had prepared sacred stones to be used by a future seer to translate the book (Alma 37:23; Mosiah 28:13).
2. A seer would use these stones by looking at or into them (Mosiah 8:13).
3. There were at least two (if not three) separate translation devices designed by God to be used for the translation of unknown languages: the two stones given to the brother of Jared (Ether 3:23), the two stones used by Mosiah (Mosiah 28:13),[7] and the single stone, Gazelem, mentioned in Alma (Alma 37:23).
4. According to Alma 37, the stones, like the other Jaredite stones, apparently functioned by shining in the darkness (though this conclusion is less certain than the first three points).

With these descriptions of translation and the seer stones from the Book of Mormon in mind, it would be helpful to turn our attention to what the witnesses and scribes of the translation of the gold plates said about the process from their experience and understanding.

During the early months of translation, Emma Hale and Martin Harris served as Joseph's principal scribes. Both provided several accounts of what it was like to be involved in the miraculous process. According to Emma, the method of translation was quite different than most modern Latter-day Saints initially assume it was or than what has been occasionally depicted in popular Latter-day Saint art. According to Emma, Joseph did not have the gold plates open in front of him as he ran his finger down the leaf, nor did he place the seer stones over the characters on the plates in order to read them. Rather, she explained, "I frequently wrote day after day, often sitting at the table close by him, he sitting with his face buried in his hat, with the stone in it, and dictating hour after hour with nothing between us."

While she made a point of saying there was no sheet or divider between them as they translated, Emma also affirmed that the plates themselves remained covered during the

HOW DID JOSEPH TRANSLATE THE BOOK OF MORMON?

process, which explains why she did not ever see the plates even though she sat across the table from Joseph while he was translating: "The plates often lay on the table without any attempt at concealment, wrapped in a small linen tablecloth, which I had given him to fold them in. I once felt of the plates, as they thus lay on the table, tracing their outline and shape. They seemed to be pliable like thick paper, and would rustle with a metallic sound when the edges were moved by the thumb, as one does sometimes thumb the edges of a book."

As odd as that explanation seems to some modern Latter-day Saints who have pictured Joseph looking directly at the plates while he translated, perhaps the most startling aspect of her description was that Joseph placed the seer stone or stones into a hat and looked into the hat while translating. This seemingly strange and unexpected description has given fodder for others to mock and belittle the process and often bewilders believers who cannot comprehend the reason for translating this way.

However, the witnesses of the translation were neither ashamed nor baffled by the use of the hat as a tool to aid the translation process. They explained that Joseph Smith needed to make the area around the seer stones dark so he could see the writing that would appear on the stones. For instance, Joseph Knight Sr., one of the few friends Joseph Smith had during this early period of translation, explained that the purpose of the hat was to block out the ambient light in the room in order to see the words as they appeared on the seer stones: "Now the way he [Joseph] translated was he put the Urim and Thummim into his hat and darkened his Eyes. Then he would take a sentence and it would appear in bright Roman letters. Then he would tell the writer and he would write it. Then that would go away [and] the next sentence would come and so on. But if it was not spelled right it would not go away till it was right. So we see it was marvelous [and] thus was the whole translated."[8]

Not only was David Whitmer one of the Three Witnesses

of the Book of Mormon, but he was also present in his father's home, where much of the translation took place, apparently without any attempt to conceal the activity. He was unaware of Joseph Knight's description of the process, yet David provided a very similar observation. He also clarified that when placing the stone in the hat, Joseph would close the brim around it to "exclude the light; and in the darkness the spiritual light would shine." Whitmer further explained that Joseph would see a character from the plates appear and

Witnesses of the translation explained that Joseph placed the seer stones in a hat to block the light, making it easier to read the writing that appeared on them.

HOW DID JOSEPH TRANSLATE THE BOOK OF MORMON?

underneath the character would be the translation in English. "Brother Joseph would," he continued, "read off the English to Oliver Cowdery, who was his principal scribe, and when it was written down and repeated to Brother Joseph to see if it was correct, then it would disappear, and another character with the interpretation would appear."[9]

While Oliver Cowdery provided a less-circulated or detailed description of the manner of translation, aside from mentioning the use of the "interpreters," one very early source relates what Cowdery apparently said of the process. When Oliver Cowdery stopped to preach at a Shaker village in Ohio in 1830 on his way to preach to the American Indians in what is today Kansas, a local Shaker leader recorded Cowdery's description of the process, which also involved Joseph Smith using a hat along with the seer stones.[10]

Cowdery also reportedly described the translation process to Josiah Jones, a local Kirtland resident and member of Baptist minister Sidney Rigdon's congregation. While many of Rigdon's parishioners followed their erstwhile preacher, embraced the Book of Mormon, and were baptized into the Church of Christ, Jones rejected the new religion. He wrote a small history of how his religious world was seemingly turned upside down overnight and included an account of his discussions with Oliver Cowdery and the other missionaries. Jones was told by the missionaries that Joseph Smith had found the gold plates and "had translated it by looking into a stone or two stones, when put into a dark place, which stones he said were found in the box with the plates. They affirmed while he looked through the stone spectacles another sat by and wrote what he told them, and thus the book was all written." After asking Cowdery to give more details of the translation process, Cowdery reportedly explained "that Smith looked into or through the transparent stones to translate what was on the plates."[11]

Martin Harris also described that as he served as a scribe for the translation of the gold plates, Joseph Smith translated by placing the seer stones into his hat.[12] Indeed, at one point, Martin apparently decided to take a bold action with regard to the stones. Finding a stone that looked similar to the one Joseph was using to translate the gold plates, Martin surreptitiously swapped out the actual stone for the one he had found. When Joseph returned to translate, he found that the replacement stone did not provide the light of revelation and translation, but rather was "dark." Martin explained that he had secretly changed out the stones in order to disprove the theory of critics who claimed Joseph was reading a manuscript tucked into the bottom of his hat instead of the words of a miraculous translation. In Martin's reasoning, were Joseph merely pretending that the words appeared on the seer stone while actually reading this hidden manuscript, Joseph would have picked up the translation right where they had left off, even with the faux seer stone. That Joseph could not translate without the sacred stone demonstrated to Harris that the work was indeed miraculous.[13]

The earliest written account of the translation of the Book of Mormon comes from Palmyra newspaper editor Jonathan Hadley, whom we met in the introduction to this book.[14] After Egbert Grandin not only refused to print the Book of Mormon but attempted to stop Martin from supporting the project, Joseph sought to employ the offices of Hadley's *Palmyra Freeman*. Hadley was Grandin's outspoken local nemesis.

Though Hadley's small-time operation could not accommodate the herculean project of printing the Book of Mormon, he went from amiable to incensed after Joseph Smith eventually agreed to terms with the recalcitrant Grandin rather than Hadley's more well-positioned friend in Rochester. Joseph had described to Hadley many of the remarkable events that had led him to the plates and how they were translated. Now Hadley determined to undermine Joseph Smith by relating the fantastical events Joseph had told him.

While antagonistic sources can clearly make a believer

uncomfortable, Hadley's account is unlike any of the others that would follow it. When Hadley wrote his piece, there were no other published accounts for him to twist and distort. Yet he knew details of how Joseph obtained the plates and their exact size and about Martin's trip to scholars in the East, as well the translation process. He could only have gotten these details from a conversation with Joseph Smith or one of the witnesses to the translation. Hadley averred he had talked to Joseph himself. Because Hadley did not think Joseph Smith or the Book of Mormon would amount to anything, he did not feel the need to embellish or distort the story of the plates. He dismissed it, for sure, but did not think the story needed to be sunk by torpedoes that were more explosive than common sense and satire. The idea was fantastical enough that no sane person would believe it—at least that's what he assumed. He published his account of the translation of the Book of Mormon in August 1829, before even the first word of the book was typeset on Grandin's press.

Hadley told his readers: "In the fall of 1827, a person by the name of Joseph Smith, of Manchester, Ontario county, reported that he had been visited in a dream by the spirit of the Almighty, and informed that in a certain hill in that town, was deposited this Golden, Bible, containing an ancient record of divine nature and origin. After having been thrice thus visited, as he states, he proceeded to the spot, and . . . the Bible was found, together with a huge pair of spectacles!" Hadley explained that Martin Harris, "an honest and industrious farmer of this town," had come to believe the story and had taken characters copied from the gold plates to the East and met with the renowned Professor Samuel Mitchell in 1828.[15]

Evidence that his knowledge came directly from Joseph Smith is further bolstered by Hadley's explanation of the gold plates, which provide the same dimensions that Joseph Smith would himself later publish but in 1829 had not ever been publicly declared: "The leaves of the Bible were plates of gold," wrote Hadley, "about eight inches long, six wide, and one eight of an inch thick, on which were engraved characters or hieroglyphics."[16] While the witnesses of the plates provided various accounts of the size of the plates, Hadley's 1829 description is the closest to the one Joseph Smith himself gave in the Wentworth letter in 1842: "These records were engraven on plates which had the appearance of gold, each plate was six inches wide and eight inches long and not quite so thick as common tin."[17]

Hadley also used the peculiar term "spectacles" to describe the device containing the two seer stones that was found with the plates. Though his recitation of Joseph's explanation of the translation was filled with incredulity, Hadley explained, "By placing the Spectacles in a hat, and looking into it, Smith could (he said so, at least) interpret these characters."[18] In Joseph Smith's first written account of the translation of the Book of Mormon, he also described the stones as "spectacles," explaining that though he felt overwhelmed by the task because he was unlearned, God had prepared the spectacles so he could translate. Thus this earliest published account of translation described the same process of placing the stones in a hat to block out the light—a description that Emma Smith, Martin Harris, David Whitmer, and Joseph Knight affirmed,

This reproduction shows what the Urim and Thummim may have looked like, based on explanations from witnesses, who often described them as "spectacles."

HOW DID JOSEPH TRANSLATE THE BOOK OF MORMON?

and one that Oliver Cowdery also described according to multiple early (1830 and 1831) sources.

At times the testimonies of these witnesses have been dismissed by modern Latter-day Saints. Confronted with these descriptions, which may be foreign to how they previously envisioned the process of translation, some have invoked the later apostasies of Martin Harris, Emma Smith, and David Whitmer in order to discard their testimonies. However, taking a much more measured approach, one can recognize that though some of these witnesses of the translation left the Church (Joseph Knight did not), none ever denied their testimony of the gold plates or of Joseph Smith as the translator of the Book of Mormon. Indeed, Latter-day Saints correctly and proudly affirm that none of the witnesses of the gold plates ever denied their testimony, despite their various apostasies. It is inconsistent to herald the witnesses' testimonies about the existence of the gold plates but then to cast aside their explanation of translation that they provided at the same time they were affirming the truthfulness of the work.

Emma was, for instance, seeking to affirm the prophetic nature of her husband. Virulent anti-Mormons of her day, such as Eber Howe, mocked the fact that Joseph translated with a seer stone and a hat. Why then would Emma describe the process of translation by repeating the description given by Howe, who hated Joseph and mocked the miracle, rather than describing how it *actually* occurred? If the process involved neither seer stones nor a hat, what motivation would Emma Smith have in making that claim while still desperately defending Joseph as a prophet? Similarly, Martin Harris affirmed his testimony both inside and outside of the Church. Did he also, though disconnected from Emma Smith, provide a false explanation that he knew was ridiculed by antagonists of the gold plates and the Book of Mormon? Indeed, Jonathan Hadley's account (the earliest) agrees with David Whitmer's (the latest). Thus, historians have concluded that the translation process must have, in some way, involved placing the stones into a hat. They have also concluded that the traditionally held notion that Joseph translated with the gold plates open in front of him has almost no support, early or late, among witnesses and scribes of the translation of the gold plates. This new understanding is reflected in the Church's Gospel Topics essay on the subject as well as in various other publications enumerated later in this chapter.

All of the witnesses of the translation describe Joseph using the seer stones or a single seer stone to translate the Book of Mormon, referring to them variously as interpreters, Urim and Thummim, spectacles, stones, crystals, etc. Several of these scribes and witnesses also affirmed that Joseph used more than one device during his translation. Emma Smith, for instance, explained, "Now the first that my husband translated, was translated by the use of the Urim, and Thummim, and that was the part that Martin Harris lost, after that he used a small stone, not exactly, black, but was rather a dark color."[19] As one of the main scribes of the translation of the gold plates, Emma's description of the translation as miraculous and involving more than one device should be taken very seriously.

Joseph Smith's possession and use of at least one separate seer stone during the translation of the Book of Mormon was once more widely understood in the Church, as a statement from Martin Harris published in the *Deseret Evening News* in 1881 indicates: He described Joseph using both the "spectacles" that had been found in the box with the gold plates as well as a separate, different stone. He stated that Joseph "possessed a seer stone, by which he was enabled to translate as well as from the Urim and Thummim, and for convenience he then used the seer stone."[20]

Earlier Church members applied the term "Gazelem" to this separate stone, invoking the name of the single stone prophesied of in Alma 37:23. Indeed, not only did Wilford Woodruff know that Joseph Smith used at least one separate seer stone in addition to the two in the spectacles, but Joseph had also shown him a single seer stone in late 1841. Wilford

HOW DID JOSEPH TRANSLATE THE BOOK OF MORMON?

later explained how Joseph obtained "the seer stone known as 'Gazelem.'" Joseph had been "shown by the Lord" where Gazelem was, "some thirty feet underground," and was able to dig down and retrieve it "under the pretense of excavating for a well."[21] President Brigham Young provided a similar explanation that "the seer stone which Joseph Smith first obtained he got in an iron kettle 15 feet underground."[22]

Wilford Woodruff supplied perhaps the most telling example of a President of the Church treating the single seer stone, still possessed by the Church, as a holy relic. In March 1888, Woodruff recorded in his journal that he "consecrated a seers stone that Joseph found in a well."[23] Two months later, Woodruff dedicated the Manti Temple on May 17, 1888. The next day, after setting apart Daniel H. Wells as the temple president, Woodruff took the seer stone (presumably the same one he had referred to two months earlier) and placed it on the altar of the temple. He recorded in his journal that he "consecrated upon the Altar the seers Stone that Joseph Smith found by Revelation some 30 feet under the Earth Carried By him through life."[24]

In the October 2015 issue of the Church magazine the *Ensign,* then–Assistant Church Historian Richard Turley and

This separate seer stone was photographed and published by Church historians in the October 2015 Ensign.

Church History Library archivists Robin Jensen and Mark Ashurst-McGee published an article describing this separate stone, with accompanying photographs, so that all Church members could have a better understanding of this seer stone. The historians explained to readers that "historical evidence shows that in addition to the two seer stones known as 'interpreters,' Joseph Smith used at least one other seer stone in translating the Book of Mormon, often placing it into a hat in order to block out light. According to Joseph's contemporaries, he did this in order to better view the words on the stone."

These detailed descriptions of Joseph Smith's translating with multiple seer stones and a hat are less well known to most Latter-day Saints than the simple, less-detailed explanation provided in Joseph Smith—History. Several modern Church leaders, however, have also referred to these early sources to explain the miraculous translation. David Whitmer's very detailed description of the process, involving the stones being placed into the hat, was highlighted by President Russell M. Nelson in 1992, while he was still an Apostle, when he was speaking to new mission presidents. He declared:

> We do have a few precious insights. David Whitmer wrote: "Joseph Smith would put the seer stone into a hat, and put his face in the hat, drawing it closely around his face to exclude the light; and in the darkness the spiritual light would shine. A piece of something resembling parchment would appear, and on that appeared the writing. One character at a time would appear, and under it was the interpretation in English. Brother Joseph would read off the English to Oliver Cowdery, who was his principal scribe, and when it was written down and repeated to Brother Joseph to see if it was correct, then it would disappear, and another character with the interpretation would appear. Thus the Book of Mormon was translated by the gift and power of God, and not by any power of man."

This address was then published in the *Ensign* in 1993.[25] Four years later, Elder Neal A. Maxwell similarly wrote about

HOW DID JOSEPH TRANSLATE THE BOOK OF MORMON?

the miracle of the Book of Mormon and its translation, using the testimonies of David Whitmer, Joseph Knight, and Martin Harris as evidence of how the process took place.[26]

In 2013, The Church of Jesus Christ of Latter-day Saints undertook efforts to help members better understand the sources surrounding the translation of the Book of Mormon. The Joseph Smith Papers, using the historical sources, provided a detailed, academic, and faithful explanation of the translation process as the scribes and witnesses understood and explained it.[27] Utilizing these resources, the Church published a Gospel Topics essay entitled "Book of Mormon Translation," which states: "Joseph Smith and his scribes wrote of two instruments used in translating the Book of Mormon. According to witnesses of the translation, when Joseph looked into the instruments, the words of scripture appeared in English."

More recently, an April 2020 *New Era* article reiterated the process of Joseph Smith using a hat along with the stones that had been prepared by God in order to translate by His gift and power. This article was published with a new image depicting Joseph Smith translating while using a hat and while the plates were covered, as Emma had described them.[28] The Church Education System institute manual now explains to students, "These accounts indicate that Joseph would place either the interpreters or the seer stone in a hat to help block out light, which allowed him to better see the words that appeared on the instrument."[29]

In 2016, Elder Dieter F. Uchtdorf took to his personal Facebook page to discuss the miracle of the translation and address the incredulity of its detractors. He was asked, "Do you really believe that Joseph Smith translated with seer stones? How would something like this be possible?" Elder Uchtdorf's response was as resounding as Wilford Woodruff's:

> I answer, "Yes! That is exactly what I believe." This was done as Joseph said: by the gift and power of God. In reality, most of us use a kind of "seer stone" every day. My mobile phone is like a "seer stone." I can get the collected

LET'S TALK ABOUT THE BOOK OF MORMON

The April 2020 edition of the New Era *published an article on the Book of Mormon translation along with this image, showing the plates covered with a cloth and Joseph translating while using a hat.*

knowledge of the world through a few little inputs. I can take a photo or a video with my phone and share it with family on the other side of our planet. I can even translate anything into or from many different languages! If I can do this with my phone, if human beings can do this with their phones or other devices, who are we to say that God could not help Joseph Smith, the Prophet of the Restoration, with his translation work? If it is possible for me to access the knowledge of the world through my phone, who can question that seer stones are impossible for God? Many religions have objects, places, and events that are sacred to them. We respect the sacred beliefs of other religions and hope to be respected for our own beliefs and what is sacred to us. We should never be arrogant, but rather polite and humble. We still should have a natural confidence, because this is the Church of Jesus Christ.[30]

More recently, President Russell M. Nelson described Joseph Smith using the seer stones by placing them in his hat to block out the light in a video interview published on the

78

Church website, entitled "The Book of Mormon Is Tangible Evidence of the Restoration."[31]

While the seer stones were apparently integral to the work, so too was Joseph Smith's spiritual preparation. If he was not properly humble and penitent, he could not translate (see chapter 7). However the process actually took place, for believers the most important aspect of the translation of the gold plates is the published Book of Mormon, which stands as not only another witness of the resurrected Jesus Christ but also as evidence of Joseph Smith's prophetic calling.

The Lord declared that the translation of the Book of Mormon was true, even as the process was still ongoing. He spoke peace to an uncertain Oliver Cowdery: "I tell thee these things as a witness unto thee—that the words or the work which thou hast been writing are true" (Doctrine and Covenants 6:17). Later, with the work nearly completed, the Lord proclaimed of the translation to the Three Witnesses, "As your Lord and your God liveth it is true" (Doctrine and Covenants 17:6). For believers, as interesting as the historical accounts of the translation of the gold plates might be, the words and teachings and doctrines of the Book of Mormon are the essential aspects of this great miracle, increasing faith in Christ, providing hope through His Atonement, and generating marvelous changes in hearts and lives.

CHAPTER 7

IMPORTANT QUESTIONS AND POSSIBLE ANSWERS

Why have I heard of the Urim and Thummim before, but not seer stones?[1]

For some members of the Church, one of the more difficult aspects of the Book of Mormon translation is the idea that Joseph Smith used other seer stones aside from the well-known Urim and Thummim. Because the canonized account of Joseph's experience in the Pearl of Great Price, Joseph Smith–History, describes the Urim and Thummim, which Joseph received with the plates, and does not mention any other stones, many Latter-day Saints assume that these two stones, bound together, were the only ones used in the translation. This conclusion is also common because the angel told Joseph that "there were two stones set in silver bows" and that one of these stones was named "Urim" while the other was named "Thummim." Similarly, the official *History of Joseph Smith* notes that when other revelations were received during this same period, they were received "through the Urim and Thummim."[2] Neither the angel nor the official history note the use of a separate seer stone. Hence, it is natural to assume that Joseph had only two stones, those that were found in the stone box with the plates, and that they were the only things he used in his seership.

That conclusion is compounded by the proliferation of Latter-day Saint art that refrains from showing even the Urim and Thummim stones being used in Joseph Smith's translation of the gold plates, let alone a separate seer stone, such as Gazelem, described in chapter 6. Though that stone is prophetically described in the Book of Mormon, there have been few popular attempts to show it. Additionally, no popular depictions attempt to show Joseph using any sacred stones to receive revelation, though in the section headings of the Doctrine and Covenants, Joseph Smith repeatedly declared that he did.

Much of this confusion and resulting discomfort with the idea that Joseph Smith had at least one other seer stone beyond those found with the plates stem from the changing terminologies used to describe these stones in the early Church. First, it may surprise many Latter-day Saints to learn that the term "Urim and Thummim," though certainly known by early members because of its biblical origins, is not used in any of the earliest documents to describe any of the seer stones, including the two stones found with the plates. The Book of Mormon too, though it discusses these sacred instruments multiple times, never uses the term "Urim and Thummim." Instead, the Book of Mormon refers to the translation instruments as "stones" or "interpreters."[3]

The two stones found with the plates were apparently most often referred to at first as "spectacles," not because of how they were used but because the two stones bound together looked similar to a giant pair of glasses. Martin Harris described the device as "two clear stones set in two rims, [that] very much resembled spectacles, only they were larger."[4] In another interview he explained that those "stones were white, like polished marble, with a few gray streaks."[5] Lucy Smith also saw the interpreters found with the plates and explained that the device "consisted of 2 smooth 3 cornered diamonds set in glass and the glass was set in silver bows connected with each other in the same way that old fashioned spectacles are made."[6]

Though Oliver Cowdery would later use the Book of Mormon term "interpreters" to describe the stones, in his earliest explanation of the translation, he too described the stones found with the plates as "spectacles." While preaching to a Shaker group in 1830, Cowdery explained that there was "in the box with the plates two transparent stones in the form of spectacles." Hyrum Smith also apparently used this description. In 1829, he wrote to his uncle Jesse Smith and witnessed to him of the truthfulness of the gold plates and the visions Joseph had experienced. A bitterly angry Jesse Smith responded with a letter filled with condemnation, dismissal, and venom for his nephews' religious claims. In his letter, Hyrum had apparently excused his father's lack of writing to Jesse because of difficulty with his eyes. Jesse saw the opening to further castigate the Palmyra Smiths and mocked in response, "If he knows not what to write, he can get your Brother's spectacles he would then be as able to dictate a letter, as Joe is to decipher hieroglyphics, if more should be wanting he can employ the same scoundrel of a scribe, and then not only the matter but manner and style would be correct."[7]

It was not only Martin Harris, Hyrum Smith, Oliver Cowdery, and Lucy Smith who compared the appearance of this device to "spectacles," but this was also the term Joseph Smith himself used in his earliest written explanation of the translation in 1832.[8] But referring to the translation devices as "spectacles" or "stones" allowed critics, such as Joseph's uncle Jesse, to easily mock the miraculous process by applying terms that had other definitions in the mundane world. By employing the biblical term "Urim and Thummim" to the stones that had been used in the translation, on the other hand, a clear distinction was made between the sacred and the profane. The Urim and Thummim in the Bible were sacred instruments, often thought to be stones, used by the high priests in Israel to receive revelation from God. A contemporary biblical commentary described the Urim and Thummim's use: "They were used in asking counsel of God in difficult and momentous cases relating to the whole state of Israel. Whether the answer was given by an audible voice or by mysterious characters on the breast plate has been a subject of unprofitable controversy."[9]

While scholars in Joseph's time debated just how the Urim and Thummim functioned, there was no debate that they were seen as holy instruments involved in revelation. Thus, by applying this biblical term to the stones Joseph had found and used, he could clearly convey to those outside the religion that the seer stones were sacred and holy, just as their Christian critics believed those in the Old Testament were. This apparently deliberate revision in nomenclature is best displayed by a January 1833 article in the Church newspaper *The Evening and the Morning Star* describing the translation of the Book of Mormon. William W. Phelps, the author, declared that Joseph translated the plates "by the gift and power of God . . . through the aid of a pair of Interpreters, or spectacles—(known, perhaps, in ancient days as Teraphim, or Urim and Thummim)."[10]

The term "Urim and Thummim" quickly thereafter came to be the accepted terminology to describe seer stones. By 1835, when Joseph described to a visitor in Kirtland what the angel had told him, he used the term "Urim and Thummim," whereas his record three years earlier used the term "spectacles." He told the visitor that the angel had said that "the Urim & Thummim was hid up with the record, and that God would give me power to translate it with the assistance of this instrument."[11] After the publication of the term in the 1835 Doctrine and Covenants, in what is now known as section 17, to describe what the Three Witnesses saw, the term was rapidly adopted. Most of the histories of the early Church were written after 1838, including the *History of Joseph Smith*, which would eventually become the *History of the Church*. By the time that later history was written in 1839, Joseph was using the term "Urim and Thummim" to reference any seer stone, not just the ones that had originally been found in the stone box with the plates.

This changing terminology makes it very difficult to determine which stone or device is being referenced since all seer stones, even the separate stone showed to Wilford Woodruff in 1841, were called "Urim and Thummim" by Joseph Smith. That Joseph came to see this term as a generic descriptor of a seer stone, rather than a reference only to the stones found in the stone box, is evident in the way he would later describe the planet upon which God resides, what the earth would become after its destruction and rebirth, and what each believer entering into the celestial kingdom would receive (see Doctrine and Covenants 130:6–9). In each case, Joseph described the very different things as "Urim and Thummim."

> Was Joseph Smith eventually able to translate the Book of Mormon without using the seer stones (i.e., Urim and Thummim/interpreters/ Gazelem)? I heard he only used the stones at first, but then stopped using them.

It is a common belief among twenty-first-century Latter-day Saints that, while Joseph Smith used the seer stones, or Urim and Thummim, to translate some of the gold plates, as he progressed spiritually, he came to the point that he no longer needed or used the holy devices. Many people today believe that at some point he received the text of the Book of Mormon by revelation through inspiration without the use of the seer stones, much like he revealed what is now the book of Moses or dozens of other revelations that he dictated. However, there is no indication from any historical record that nineteenth-century Latter-day Saints similarly believed that Joseph did not use the seer stones to translate the entirety of the Book of Mormon.

While we can never be certain how the entire miraculous process took place (we do not, for instance, have a daily log entry that states, "We used the interpreters today"), we can use the sources we do have to make the most likely conclusion. We do not know of any witnesses of the translation, early or late in the process, or close associates of Joseph Smith who claimed he translated the gold plates at any point without the use of the seer stones. All of the witnesses of the translation explained that Joseph Smith used the interpreters or a separate single seer stone to translate. Though the witnesses refer to the stones in several different ways, they all agree that a stone was used in the translation.

Additionally, while Joseph Smith did not provide many details of the translation process, when he did explain the miracle to others, he repeatedly described his use of the stones to translate the plates. In his earliest account, Joseph connected the sacred stones with translation directly. After lamenting that he could not possibly translate the ancient record because he was not learned, Joseph affirmed that the "Lord had prepared spectacles" to accomplish the translation.[12]

Several years later, in 1835, when an ostentatious visitor to Kirtland proclaimed himself to be a prophet, Joseph responded by describing the miracles of the First Vision and the translation of the Book of Mormon. Joseph recounted that when the angel told him of the gold plates, he had also declared that "the Urim and Thumim, was hid up with the record, and that God would give [him] power to translate it, with the assistance of this instrument."[13]

In 1838, as editor of the *Elders' Journal*, published by the Church in Far West, Joseph again explained that he used the seer stones to translate the record. He told readers that after the angel showed him where the plates were buried, "I obtained them, and the Urim and Thummim with them; by the means of which, I translated the plates; and thus came the book of Mormon."[14]

In the famous Wentworth letter, in which Joseph Smith outlined the Articles of Faith of the Church, he also gave a brief history of his visions and the translation of the Book of Mormon. Joseph wanted the information in this letter to be published to the world, and when it became apparent that such a publication would not be forthcoming, Joseph published it himself in the *Times and Seasons* newspaper in Nauvoo. Describing the translation process to the public, he stated, "Through the medium of the Urim and Thummim I translated the record by the gift, and power of God"; he never once added that there was any other means by which he translated the Book of Mormon.[15]

In 1842, in his official history that he also published to the world in the *Times and Seasons,* and which would later be canonized as scripture, Joseph similarly described the translation as being performed by use of the sacred stones. He said the angel told him "that there were two stones . . . deposited with the plates, and the possession and use of these stones was what constituted seers in ancient or former times, and that God had prepared them for the purpose of translating the book."[16]

Joseph's revelations attest to this fact also. The revelation now known as Doctrine and Covenants 10 chastised Joseph for his part in the loss of the stolen 116 pages. The revelation was intended to be published to the Church and world in the 1833 Book of Commandments. However, a mob destroyed the printing press just before the book's publication was completed, preventing it from gaining its anticipated circulation. In that 1833 published version, the chastisement of Joseph Smith read in part, "Because you delivered up so many writings, which you had power to translate."[17] But when the revelation was again published two years later, in 1835, in the first edition of the Doctrine and Covenants, the same sentence was edited to emphasize the method of translation: "Because you delivered up those writings which you had power given unto you to translate, *by the means of the Urim and Thummim*."[18]

If none of the scribes of the translation, nor Joseph Smith himself, ever claimed Joseph translated the gold plates without the use of seer stones, where does this present-day misunderstanding come from? The idea that Joseph did not always use seer stones likely has some genesis in modernist thinking, which feels uncomfortable with unexplained phenomena in general, let alone the use of holy instruments to receive revelation or perform miracles. While the Book of Mormon prophets regularly used sacred objects—from seer stones to translate Jaredite records to the Liahona to receive written revelation and direction from God—such types of physical and mystical objects do not resonate with most people living in the twenty-first century. Instead, they are often more comfortable perceiving revelation as something that is received only in someone's mind, without the aid of external instruments.

This mistaken view of Joseph's use of seer stones is further ensconced because of a misapplication of an Orson Pratt quote that was given four decades after the Book of Mormon translation had been completed. Orson was not affiliated with the Smiths while the translation was taking place but joined the Church shortly after it was organized in 1830. In an 1871 meeting of the School of the Prophets in Salt Lake City, Orson recounted a conversation he had held with Joseph Smith about the Bible translation, which took place sometime between 1831 and 1833. Orson Pratt recalled that he had observed that "as Joseph used the Urim and Thummim in the translation of the Book of Mormon, he wondered why he did not use it in the translation of the New Testament. Joseph explained to him that the experience he had acquired while translating the Book of Mormon by the use of the Urim and Thummim had rendered him so well acquainted with the spirit of Revelation and Prophecy, that in the translating of the New Testament he did not need the aid that was necessary in the 1st instance."[19]

While there are surprisingly few contemporary sources that describe the details of Joseph's years-long effort to translate the Bible, none of them reference Joseph Smith using seer stones to perform that work. Similarly, there are far fewer references to Joseph using seer stones to receive revelations in general in the years following the translation of the Book of Mormon.

For those grappling with the oddity of Joseph using an external object, and a stone at that, to translate the gold plates or receive revelation from God, Orson Pratt's report on the later Bible translation provides an avenue of escape from the difficulty of trying to reconcile their expectations with actual events as recorded by witnesses. With Orson's quote about the Bible translation, some may conclude that Joseph only used seer stones during a time when he was not fully developed as a seer. As his understanding and abilities grew, his need for the seer stones ebbed in favor of direct revelation—a concept more relatable to twenty-first century Latter-day Saints.

While easily digestible, however, there are some problems associated with this explanation of progressive abilities rendering the seer stones unnecessary during the Book of Mormon translation. First, Pratt did not claim Joseph Smith ever translated the Book of Mormon without the Urim and Thummim; in fact, he reiterated the opposite—that Joseph had translated the gold plates with the sacred stones. Pratt's entire conversation with Joseph is based on the premise that Joseph had translated the gold plates with those stones—hence the reason he asked why Joseph translated the Bible without them.[20]

Second, and more broadly, the assumption that seer stones were useful only in Joseph's early, limited state as a seer seems to conflict with the description of seers given in the Book of Mormon. The Book of Mormon prophets also used stones to translate languages. Was Mosiah also in the formative years of his seership when he used sacred stones to translate the Jaredite records? (see Mosiah 28:11–14). When the Lord presented the brother of Jared with the two stones for the purpose of translating the record he had created, did the Lord simply mean them to be a temporary aid to a fledgling future seer? (see Ether 2:22–28). Further, as Joseph revealed in the book of Abraham, Abraham too possessed and used a Urim and Thummim. Abraham explained that the device had been given to him by the Lord and, through it, Abraham both saw many wonders of the heavens and received communication from the Lord (see Abraham 3:1–4). Rather than being novel instruments designed to help the weak or uncertain, seer stones, as testified in revealed scripture, are a regular part of God's method of communicating with His chosen seers and revelators.

Of course, seers do not need to utilize sacred stones in order to be seers. Their calling and keys come from the Lord, independent of any external devices, just as Lehi was a seer long before the Liahona was discovered outside of the family tent. Joseph received revelation via visions, angelic visitations, and inspiration, as well as through the seer stones. The historical record clearly indicates that Joseph used the seer stones less often after the translation of the Book of Mormon was completed. Thus Pratt's much later observation about the Bible translation fits well into the documented behavior of Joseph Smith.

Still, though it seems evident that Joseph used the stones much less often after the translation of the Book of Mormon, he did still continue to use them, albeit very sporadically. Ironically, one of the strongest pieces of evidence that Joseph Smith continued to receive revelations through the seer stones after the publication of the Book of Mormon also comes from Orson Pratt; Joseph Smith dictated a revelation directed to Orson, now known as Doctrine and Covenants 34. Shortly after his conversion, Orson was reportedly anxious to know

> what his mission was and would be, and at Peter Whitmer Sr's residence he asked Joseph whether he could not ascertain what his mission was, and Joseph answered him that he would see, & asked Pratt and John Whitmer to go upstairs with him, and on arriving there Joseph produced a small stone called a seer stone, and putting it into a Hat soon commenced speaking and asked Elder P[ratt] to write as he would speak, but being too young and timid and feeling his unworthiness he asked whether Bro. John W[hitmer] could not write it, and the Prophet said that he could: Then came the revelation.[21]

Such an experience, if accurate, undercuts the idea that Joseph progressed to the point that he no longer needed to use the stones to translate the Book of Mormon since, more than a year after the Book of Mormon translation had been completed, Joseph used a stone to dictate the revelation declaring the Lord's mission for Orson Pratt. For whatever reason Joseph Smith used the seer stone to receive that revelation, Pratt affirms that he did.

Though his account also looks back decades earlier, Edward Stevenson too affirmed an experience in which Joseph Smith used the seer stones years after the translation of the gold plates had been completed. Joseph, apparently in late 1837 or early 1838, borrowed *Fox's Book of Martyrs* from Stevenson's mother and pledged to return it when they all arrived in

Missouri. Upon returning the book to the Stevensons as promised, Joseph told them he had, "by the aid of the Urim and Thummim, seen those martyrs, and they were honest, devoted followers of Christ, according to the light they possessed, and they will be saved."[22]

In December 1841, Wilford Woodruff excitedly wrote in his journal of an experience he had just had with the Prophet Joseph Smith. In a meeting with other Apostles, Joseph had unfolded unto them "many glorious things of the kingdom of God," and Woodruff exulted that he also "had the privilege of seeing for the first time in my day the URIM & THUMMIM," indicating that Joseph had shown him one or more seer stones he still had in his possession.[23] This profound experience, along with Joseph's other teachings and revelations, still resonated with Woodruff two months later. He confided in his journal:

> It is truly interesting, edifying, and glorious to contemplate the great & mighty work which God has set his hand to establish in these last days by revealing the fullness of the everlasting gospel as recorded in the Book of Mormon and establishing his church and kingdom as at the beginning, which is according to the order of heaven with Seers, Prophets Apostles, Elders, Priests, Bishops, Teachers, revelation, administering of angels gifts, graces, knowledge, wisdom, tongues, healings, etc. Truly the Lord has raised up Joseph the Seer of the seed of Abraham out of the loins of ancient Joseph, and is now clothing him with mighty power and wisdom and knowledge which is more clearly manifest and felt in the midst of his intimate friends than any other class of mankind.[24]

Woodruff came away from the experience believing that the seer stones had also played a role in the translation of the book of Abraham, concluding, "The Lord is blessing Joseph with power to reveal the mysteries of the kingdom of God, to translate through the Urim and Thummim ancient records and hieroglyphics as old as Abraham or Adam, which causes our hearts to burn within us while we behold their glorious truths opened unto us."[25]

At any rate, throughout Joseph's life, whether he was showing the seer stones to Wilford Woodruff or explaining to non–Latter-day Saints how he translated the Book of Mormon, Joseph neither attempted to hide his use of the Urim and Thummim nor claimed the translation was done in some other way. Far from moving away from the idea of seer stones, Joseph's teachings and revelations expounded upon the centrality of sacred seer stones in Latter-day Saint theology.

In 1843, for example, Joseph taught that the place God resided "was a great Urim and Thummim." Further, he explained that "this earth, in its sanctified and immortal state, will be made like unto crystal and will be a Urim and Thummim to the inhabitants who dwell thereon." Linking these sacred stones to both the Bible and those who would be exalted, he further declared that "the white stone mentioned in Revelation 2:17, will become a Urim and Thummim to each individual who receives one, whereby things pertaining to a higher order of kingdoms will be made known; and a white stone is given to each of those who come into the celestial kingdom, whereon is a new name written, which no man knoweth save he that receiveth it. The new name is the key word." These teachings were later canonized in section 130:8–11 of the Doctrine and Covenants.

Because recorded instances of Joseph Smith using the seer stones are very infrequent in his later years, it makes sense to speculate that Joseph did not use them in the same way in the years that followed the translation of the Book of Mormon. However, no sources, early or late, reference him translating the Book of Mormon in any other way than the way he described. In his public, published accounts of the translation, Joseph maintained he had performed the miracle by the use of the seer stones, which is precisely how the scribes and witnesses of the translation also described the process.

After Joseph Smith's death, Oliver Cowdery, who had

earlier apostatized, repented and returned to the Church. His powerful testimony to a congregation of Latter-day Saints affirms both the miraculous nature of the translation and the use of the sacred stones to perform it:

> I wrote with my own pen the entire Book of Mormon (save a few pages) as it fell from the lips of the prophet as he translated it by the gift and power of God, by means of the Urim and Thummim, or as it is called by that book – holy Interpreters. I beheld with my eyes and handled with my hands the gold plates from which it was translated. I also beheld the Interpreters. That book is true. Sidney Rigdon did not write it. Mr. Spaulding did not write it. I wrote it myself as it fell from the lips of the prophet. It contains the everlasting gospel. And came in fulfillment of the revelations of John where he says he seen an angel come with the everlasting gospel to preach to every nation tongue and people. It contains principles of salvation. And if you will walk by its light and obey its precepts you will be saved in the everlasting kingdom of God.[26]

While it is entirely possible some of the translation was performed without the use of the sacred stones prepared for that purpose, none of our existing records provide evidence for that assertion.

Why do we use the word *translation* to describe the miraculous process?

This question emerges because Joseph Smith declared that he "translated by the Gift and Power of God" and the historical records describe him reading words from a seer stone as part of the process of translating the Book of Mormon. In other words, he did not translate from his own understanding of Reformed Egyptian. This distinction demonstrates that the process was drastically different from how translation occurs academically. Joseph identified God's power as the source from which the translation from one language to another occurred, and he participated in the process as the prophetic figure who had been given the "gift" to reveal the translation. This does not imply that he was directly involved in finding equivalent meaning between two different languages but rather that his role in the process of translation was to act as a seer or prophet (like Mosiah II) who received the translation from God. His gift relied directly upon the power of God. Indeed, the translation would have been impossible without it.

Joseph and his colleagues also used the word *translate* to emphasize that the text of the Book of Mormon came from the gold plates. Some might wonder if terms like *revelation*, *vision*, or *inspiration* might be better at representing the process, but Joseph and his colleagues insisted on the term *translation*. They were aware of the difference between his translations and his revelations; this distinction is clear because he did not call the book of Moses a translation, and he differentiated between Doctrine and Covenants 7, which was a translation, and other Doctrine and Covenants sections that were considered revelations, not translations from an original record. On the other hand, he did call the book of Abraham and the Book of Mormon translations from ancient records. Joseph Smith apparently used the term *translation* to describe the change from one language and record to another language and record. This usage was meant to demonstrate the origins of the original text and the process by which it came forth.

Is there textual or historical evidence to demonstrate that Joseph Smith dictated the Book of Mormon?

Emeritus linguistics professor Royal Skousen is the founding scholar of the Critical Text Project for the Book of Mormon at Brigham Young University and a member of the Joseph Smith Papers Project. His research represents the most comprehensive study of the early manuscripts of the Book of Mormon. Drawing on a combination of historical sources and with a detailed focus on scribal errors, he argues that the original manuscript exhibits signs of dictation, thus indicating Joseph Smith did in fact read words from a seer stone during the translation of the Book of Mormon. Specifically, the original manuscript features dictation blocks of twenty to thirty words. He also argues that Oliver Cowdery and others exhibited scribal anticipation when they recorded Joseph's dictation. What he means by this is that words were often skipped or placed too early in the sentence by his scribes (see Alma 56:41; 2 Nephi 25:6). Skousen explains that at times it seems that Joseph spoke too fast for the scribe to record his dictation. The scribes did not appear to have a text they were copying from. If Joseph Smith had a copy of the text or a compilation of written texts that had already been prepared, the earliest manuscripts would not have these signs of dictation.[27]

Samuel Brown, another Latter-day Saint scholar who has examined the method of translation, has argued that Skousen cannot demonstrate sufficiently with his evidence that Joseph was *reading* the words he was speaking. Brown instead argues that Joseph did not read the text and that he had more choice in the words he dictated. His research claims that the text of the Book of Mormon includes numerous missteps that indicate flexibility in the dictation of the text. He explains that the missteps demonstrate that Joseph would verbally communicate a passage from the Book of Mormon, then without retracting that passage from the manuscript, say something different, or even opposite (hence, a "misstep"). For example, Mosiah 7:8 reads, "And they stood before the king, and were permitted, ['were permitted' is the misstep] or rather commanded, that they should answer the questions which he should ask them." (See also 2 Nephi 33:8; Mosiah 2:31; Alma 2:34; 37:21; 54:5; 3 Nephi 7:7; 3:14; Helaman 3:33.) Brown argues that these examples are evidence that, at least in these instances, Joseph was not reading. Brown instead advocates that Joseph could have received the text he dictated through multiple revelatory means, such as visions or inspiration.[28]

The counterargument to Brown's research is that it is possible that the original author of the text on the plates (Mormon or otherwise) made the misstep. If an error was engraved in metal, there would have been no way to erase it, offering a

IMPORTANT QUESTIONS AND POSSIBLE ANSWERS

good reason for why the apparent missteps are present in the Book of Mormon.

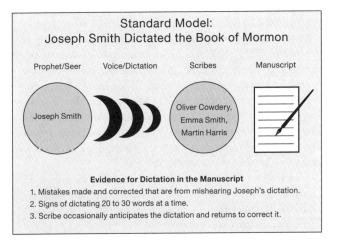

Standard Model: Joseph Smith Dictated the Book of Mormon

Prophet/Seer — Joseph Smith

Voice/Dictation

Scribes — Oliver Cowdery, Emma Smith, Martin Harris

Manuscript

Evidence for Dictation in the Manuscript
1. Mistakes made and corrected that are from mishearing Joseph's dictation.
2. Signs of dictating 20 to 30 words at a time.
3. Scribe occasionally anticipates the dictation and returns to correct it.

If Joseph Smith left no personal records indicating that he saw words on his Urim and Thummim, why trust the witnesses of the translation, who claimed that he did see words on the seer stones?

It is commonly stated that Joseph Smith never told anyone how he translated the Book of Mormon. This is true to some extent. He did not give a full analysis of what he experienced at the moment of translation, but he did allude to the basic mechanics of the process, as we have demonstrated elsewhere in this book. Historical sources describe the mechanics of translation to include the following: Joseph (1) looked into a hat, where the Urim and Thummim or seer stone was placed. He then (2) verbally delivered the text of the Book of Mormon to a scribe.

Most theories of translation wonder about what happened in between steps one and two. The most common historical answer is that he read words that appeared on his seer stones, as his scribes said that he did. The witnesses of the translation and the scribes certainly believed Joseph was miraculously reading words off of the sacred instruments. Yet because Joseph did not expressly say that understanding in any available historical statements, some have proffered other theories about what might have happened while Joseph was looking at the stones. They argue that, rather than reading words from a Urim and Thummim stone, Joseph received revelation in his mind or perhaps through a waking vision in which he mentally saw the scenes of the Book of Mormon and then found a way to explain them via his own volition. Some argue that the hat was therefore used to quiet Joseph's mind and prepare him for the vision or revelation rather than to read words from the stone, as the witnesses later asserted.

In addition to the historical theory of translation (advanced in this book), the following are theories of translation that include a divine element. Of course, those who reject Joseph Smith's prophetic truth claims also reject the divinity of the Book of Mormon, alleging that he or someone else created the text, either drawing from other sources or his own imagination without any divine inspiration, or as is most commonly argued, a mixture of both.

1. *Reading: When Joseph looked into the hat, he read the words of the translation from something inside the hat.* This theory emphasizes Royal Skousen's evidence that Joseph Smith was reading something, though it does not determine what he was reading. Skeptics might use this evidence to demonstrate that he had placed in the hat pages torn from the Bible or a prepared manuscript that he had produced before the performance of the translation with his scribes. Historical sources from the witnesses, however, argue that the words of the Book of Mormon came directly from his Urim and Thummim.

2. *Revelation: When Joseph looked into the hat, he received revelation from God.* God delivered the words of the translation directly to his mind, instead of on a seer stone. That inspiration could have been exact words

(making this theory very similar to the one that he read the words from the seer stone) but could have also been less precise. Joseph might have received inspired thoughts or narratives that he was expected to articulate in his own words.

3. *Visions: Joseph received visions as he looked into his hat.* These could have been visions of the text, visions of the specific events described on the gold plates, or even grand all-seeing visions, like Nephi's vision. This theory is interesting and may actually subsume the theory that he read words from the Urim and Thummim, since the glowing words could be described as a vision. In other words, the Urim and Thummim could have served as a screen for Joseph's vision of the translated words. If instead Joseph had visions of the actual events of the Book of Mormon, he would have had a firsthand perspective of the historical and contextual setting of the Book of Mormon narratives and then related those to his scribe.

Theories of Divine Translation		
Reading	Revelation	Visions
Joseph read words, such as those that miraculously appeared on the seer stones, which he dictated to his scribes.	Joseph received divine revelation in the form of inspired words, thoughts, and narratives which he dictated to his scribes.	Joseph had a miraculous vision and related what he saw to his scribe. In his vision, he perhaps saw the text itself or the narrative, or he had a panoptic vision of the events.

That there are different theories of translation stems from the fact that Joseph Smith never left a personal account of seeing words on his Urim and Thummim. Hence, while still maintaining that God was ultimately responsible for the translation of the Book of Mormon, individuals often speculatively explore what might have occurred while Joseph Smith gazed into his hat or even suggest that he perhaps translated without any external object at all. Despite these various theories, the Gospel Topics Essay published by The Church of Jesus Christ of Latter-day Saints asserts primarily the historical position of this book: "The scribes and others who observed the translation left numerous accounts that give insight into the process. Some accounts indicate that Joseph studied the characters on the plates. Most of the accounts speak of Joseph's use of the Urim and Thummim (either the interpreters or the seer stone), and many accounts refer to his use of a single stone. According to these accounts, Joseph placed either the interpreters or the seer stone in a hat, pressed his face into the hat to block out extraneous light, and read aloud the English words that appeared on the instrument."[29]

Is it possible Joseph Smith was creatively involved in the translation?

Active Latter-day Saint scholars Royal Skousen and Blake Ostler faithfully asked the question, "How much was Joseph Smith creatively involved in the production of the Book of Mormon text?" The reading model is an argument, within itself, that demonstrates that Joseph did not have any creative involvement. It does this by emphasizing God's tight control over the translated text. Joseph delivered only exact words on the Urim and Thummim. Theories of translation in which he was given the text by revelation, inspiration, or a combination of several methods give Joseph some credit for the text of the Book of Mormon, or at least require his creative involvement with direction from God. Skousen has created a helpful scale for describing Joseph's involvement: iron clad, tight control, and loose control.

Skousen explains, "There appear to be three possible kinds of control over the dictation of the Book of Mormon text:

1. *Loose control:* Ideas were revealed to Joseph Smith, and he put the ideas into his own language (a theory advocated by many Book of Mormon scholars over the years).

IMPORTANT QUESTIONS AND POSSIBLE ANSWERS

2. *Tight control:* Joseph Smith saw specific words written out in English and read them off to the scribe—the accuracy of the resulting text depending on the carefulness of Joseph Smith and his scribe.
3. *Iron-clad control:* Joseph Smith (or the interpreters themselves) would not allow any error made by the scribe to remain (including the spelling of common words).

One can also conceive of mixtures of these different kinds of control. For instance, one might argue for tight control over the spelling of specific names, but loose control over the English phraseology itself."[30]

There are others who reject the divine origin of the text and argue either that Joseph compiled the Book of Mormon text himself, or with help from his friends and family, or that he found someone else's manuscript and fraudulently claimed that manuscript was the translated text. In addition to these secular arguments, which lack any direct evidence and are completely antithetical to the witness and scribe statements, one scholar, Ann Taves, has attempted to argue that perhaps Joseph Smith fell into an unconscious, trance-like state wherein he began auto writing the text. Taves uses the example of Helen Schucman as an example of someone who appeared to produce text while unconscious. Without acknowledging any miraculous or divine involvement, this argument allows for Joseph to both be the author of the text and honestly claim that the words came from some other place.

Still, Taves's explanation rejects all of the witness and scribal statements, none of which describe anything like unconscious automatic writing and provide multiple explanations of the process that directly contradict her explanation. The historical record, from those who witnessed the translation, explicitly argues for the translation's divine origins, not for its secular compilation or human creation.

What was God's translation method?

To "translate" something is to literally change it. If someone were to translate a large volume like the Book of Mormon from one language to another with only word-for-word translations, it would be unreadable, with nonsensical sentence structures and inappropriate meaning. All translation is done based on a theory or method of changing one language to another language. Scholars thinking about the theory of the translation of the Book of Mormon, such as Brant Gardner, have taken this into account. The chart below shows a few examples of how scholars have argued God may have worked through Joseph Smith to translate the gold plates.

The Divine Translation: Egyptian/Reformed Egyptian to English

One to One	The Book is a linguistic translation (matching word for word, sentence structure, and meaning) of the reformed Egyptian on the plates.
Sociocultural	The Book translates the reformed Egyptian from the translator's perspective, reflecting the society and culture of the nineteenth century reader to understand an ancient culture and society.
Interpretive	The Book was translated with little regard to exact linguistic meaning found in the reformed Egyptian, instead focusing on meaning and communication.
Literary	The Book was translated as a piece of literature, not a linguistic project. It captures the energy behind language and efficaciously translates that into words.
Symbolic	The Book was translated semiotically to capture the relationship between signs and signification. Each sign has a unique sociocultural context.
Religious	The primary focus of the translation was religious and spiritual enlightenment, not historical, linguistic, or cultural.

IMPORTANT QUESTIONS AND POSSIBLE ANSWERS

What other theories of translation have been proposed?

Royal Skousen has provided a standard model of translation for Latter-day Saints, but John Welch has also produced a popular apologetic approach to the translation, based primarily upon the translation being a demonstrable miracle. There are numerous translation theories that have been proposed, including some that emphasize geography and lands of the Book of Mormon. Scholars in several different disciplines have proposed theories, and the chart below lists some of them. Some theories reject the potential of divine involvement, providing instead a naturalistic explanation. Those naturalistic explanations, such as William Davis's and Ann Taves's, are obviously less convincing to Latter-day Saints because the theories reject the divine origins of the Book of Mormon.

Examples of Recent Translations Theories

Translation Theory	Author	Description	Discipline	Involvement
Textual or Linguistic	Royal Skousen	Joseph miraculously read the translation from seer stones.	Linguistics	Tight control
Metaphysical	Samuel Brown	Joseph received the text through visions and other spiritual experiences.	Theology, culture	Loose control
Realist or Naturalist	William Davis	Joseph was capable of producing the text himself.	History, memory studies	Secular
Anti-Naturalist	John Welch	Joseph and his colleagues were incapable of producing the Book of Mormon. Translation occurred in seventy-two days or fewer.	History, theology	Tight control

Translation Theory	Author	Description	Discipline	Involvement
Cognitive	Brant Gardner	The text came as a series of thoughts and language, emerging first mentally.	Psychology, Meso-American studies	Tight or loose control
Automatic Writing	Ann Taves	The text came to Joseph unconsciously, automatically, and rapidly. This is a naturalist explanation.	Religious studies, social sciences	Secular

Did a sheet separate Joseph Smith and his scribes, hiding the plates during the translation?

Some Latter-day Saints see artists' portrayals of the translation process and notice that most depictions do not show a sheet separating Joseph Smith and the plates from Oliver Cowdery, Martin Harris, Emma Smith, or some other scribe. It is, however, widely believed that the translation took place with a blanket or sheet drawn across the room, with Joseph on one side and the scribe on the other. While there are several reasons for this belief, most of the sources of this explanation are from antagonistic non-eyewitnesses who gave their accounts years after the events took place.

None of the eyewitnesses to the translation described a sheet separating Joseph Smith and the scribes. Martin Harris's detailed accounts of the translation from the seer stones do not include a description of a shielding sheet blocking his view of what was going on. Similarly, Oliver Cowdery made no mention of a divider between the two men. Indeed, Emma Smith appeared to specifically refute this idea. In an interview with her son Joseph Smith III, she explained that she "wrote day after day, often sitting at the table close by him, he sitting with his face buried in his hat, with the stone in it, and dictating hour after hour with *nothing* between us."[31]

If the witnesses did not relate that a sheet hung between

Joseph and his scribes, from where does this lingering idea originate? In 1834, the first comprehensive anti-Mormon book, *Mormonism Unvailed*, was published by the editor of the *Painesville Telegraph*, Eber D. Howe. Howe eschewed what he saw as the excesses of the revivals that had cropped up during the Second Great Awakening and had mockingly criticized the first Latter-day Saint missionaries who had arrived in the area with Oliver Cowdery in late 1830 as "pretenders."

As the movement gained strength and Kirtland became the headquarters of the fledgling but rapidly expanding Church, Howe expanded his published attacks, labeling Martin Harris "an imposter" and republishing many critiques of the Book of Mormon and its believers from other newspapers and preachers.[32] Howe's problems with the sect became much more personal after his wife, Sophia Howe, joined the Church and even donated money to the cause of the redemption of Zion.[33]

Howe filled his book with affidavits of residents of New York and Pennsylvania who belittled and rejected the miraculous claims of Joseph Smith. Responding to the believers' story of Professor Charles Anthon certifying the characters of the Book of Mormon as genuine, Howe solicited Anthon's own explanation of events. Given how reviled "Mormonism" was by Americans, it is not surprising then that Anthon tried to distance himself as much as possible from the founding of the Church of Christ and the Book of Mormon.

As part of his dismissal, Anthon explained Harris had been shielded from what was really going on since Joseph had copied characters from the plates and translated some of them while a curtain separated the two of them. By pointing out that Martin could not even see Joseph as he interacted with the plates, this explanation was clearly designed to mock how easily Martin had been duped.[34]

Almost a decade after Howe published the Anthon rebuttal describing a "curtain" being drawn across the room, an Episcopalian minister claimed to have had a lengthy conversation about the gold plates and the characters with Martin

Harris many years earlier. Reverend John A. Clark angrily derided the Book of Mormon as "an imposture" and claimed that Sidney Rigdon had been involved in writing it, a claim not supported by any historical evidence. As part of his dismissal, taking a cue from Eber Howe's attempt to portray Harris as a hoodwinked fool, Clark also claimed that Harris had been shielded from the translation process: "The way that Smith made his transcripts and translations for Harris was the following. Although in the same room, a thick curtain or blanket was suspended between them, and Smith concealed behind the blanket, pretended to look through his spectacles, or transparent stones, and would then write down or repeat what he saw, which, when repeated aloud, was written down by Harris, who sat on the other side of the suspended blanket."[35]

Clark's caustic reflection was clearly influenced by Eber Howe's work, making his account even more problematic when compared with the accounts of Martin Harris himself. Even if both Anthon and Clark accurately reported being told about the use of a blanket or curtain, both men interacted with Martin in early 1828, when very little, if any, of the translation of the gold plates had taken place. If Martin did in fact speak about a curtain separating them, it would have been in relation to copying characters off of the plates rather than the translation of the book itself.[36]

David Whitmer attempted to settle this matter in an interview published later in his life. The interviewer related Whitmer's explanation:

> In order to give privacy to the proceeding, a blanket, which served as a portiere, was stretched across the family living room to shelter the translators and the plates from the eyes of any who might call at the house while the work was in progress. This, Mr. Whitmer says, was the only use made of the blanket, and it was not for the purpose of concealing the plates or the translator from the eyes of the amanuenses [scribes]. In fact, Smith was at no time hidden

from his collaborators, and the translation was performed in the presence of not only the persons mentioned, but of the entire Whitmer household and several of Smith's relatives besides.[37]

If Joseph Smith did not look at the plates as he translated, why did he even need to get the plates at all?

Because many Latter-day Saints have always envisioned Joseph Smith translating with his hand running across the characters on the gold plates, the process described by the witnesses and scribes is sometimes a bit shocking. Since they all mentioned that Joseph looked at and read words off of the stones prepared by God, apparently after they were placed in a hat, it appears that Joseph did not directly look at the plates during the translation. If there was no sheet or blanket between Joseph and his scribes, then the fact the plates were themselves covered during the translation becomes obvious. Emma served as a scribe at the same table with Joseph yet did not see the plates themselves, only the cloth they were wrapped in. Martin Harris served as a scribe for months, but as of March of 1829, as the text of Doctrine and Covenants 5 confirms, he had not seen the gold plates yet.

The answer to the question "Could God have given the text of the Book of Mormon to Joseph Smith without Joseph's possession of the plates?" is of course yes. God in His omnipotence can deliver His word in many miraculous ways. He certainly could have led Nephi in the wilderness without the Liahona, and Jesus could have easily healed the blind man without first putting clay on his eyes. In these cases, even though God had the power to perform the miracle without an external, physical instrument, He chose to use an object as part of the miracle.

We do not know what it took for Joseph to be spiritually prepared to translate the gold plates in the way God intended. Not only did Joseph struggle for years to purify himself to be able to even obtain the plates, he also had them in his possession for months before he began to translate them. During that time Joseph studied the characters and attempted to create an alphabet of them.[38] Perhaps this was a necessary time of preparation.

We know that the translation was not merely a matter of physical mechanics from the story David Whitmer related about a time Joseph was not sufficiently spiritually prepared to resume the translation as he normally would:

> One morning when he was getting ready to continue the translation, something went wrong about the house and he was put out about it. Something that Emma, his wife, had done. Oliver and I went upstairs, and Joseph came up soon after to continue the translation, but he could not do anything. He could not translate a single syllable. He went downstairs, out into the orchard, and made supplication to the Lord; was gone about an hour – came back to the house, asked Emma's forgiveness, and then came upstairs where we were and the translation went on all right. He could do nothing save he was humble and faithful.[39]

David Whitmer again stressed this fact in a book he published a few years later. He said there were times when Joseph went to translate, placed the stone into the hat, and yet would be unable to translate. "He told us," Whitmer explained, "that his mind dwelt too much on earthly things" and that was preventing him from translating as he normally would. Whitmer said that "when in this condition he [Joseph] would go out and pray, and when he became sufficiently humble before God, he could then proceed with the translation."[40]

In any case, the possession of the plates seems to have been directly connected with Joseph's role as a seer. When he incurred divine displeasure because of his repeated requests to allow Martin Harris to take the manuscript pages to show family members, part of Joseph's punishment consisted of having both the seer stones and the gold plates taken from him for a time. It is entirely possible that, however the miracle actually took place, the plates needed to be in possession of the seer for the translation to occur, whether he was looking at them or not.

The plates also served as a tangible, physical witness that the fantastic work Joseph was engaged in was not merely some flight of fancy or misunderstood dream. It is relatively easy for critics to dismiss a person's revelatory claims. People need not be deliberately deceitful to believe that the dream they had was in fact some kind of communication from God or that their powerful personal impression came from a divine source. It is clear from the totality of Joseph Smith's life and writings that he sincerely believed he had been called by God to bring about the Restoration. But unlike many other religious figures, Joseph claimed a divine calling that was buttressed by the existence of gold plates. While one can argue someone could confuse a powerful dream for a miraculous manifestation, no one can confuse whether or not they have dozens of pounds of metal plates—filled with ancient, indecipherable characters—on the table in front of them.

The gold plates physically manifested to Joseph and all of the scribes and witnesses that this endeavor was not merely a misguided dream or even the influence of some evil spirit on Joseph. The gold plates connected the present to the ancient past, declaring via Mormon and Moroni's work the reality of these ancient peoples and prophets. The gold plates were and continue to be the physical proof of Jesus's visit to the Americas and, consequently, of His Resurrection.

CONCLUSION

The scribes and witnesses of the translation of the Book of Mormon spoke and wrote of the miracles they witnessed multiple times throughout their lives. Their various accounts include several repeated elements: They saw Joseph using seer stones, either the ones found together with the plates or a separate single stone Joseph had found earlier in his life. They described Joseph placing those stones in his hat and looking into the hat to commence speaking the translated words. Several believed, either because Joseph explained it to them or because they each independently came to the same supposition, that Joseph placed the stones into the hat in order to make the area around the stones dark enough to see words that divinely appeared on them. They did not believe in the reality and divinity of the Book of Mormon *in spite of* the fact Joseph translated with these sacred stones; they believed *because of* that very miracle. As they heard the words of the Book of Mormon fall from his lips, they were certain that the words were the translation of the engravings on the gold plates Joseph had received from an angel. Several of those witnesses saw not only the plates but also the angel. As David Whitmer concluded, "Thus was the Book of Mormon translated by the gift and power of God and not by any power of man."[1]

Believing Latter-day Saints are well aware that most people reject the divine origin of the Book of Mormon and Joseph Smith as the seer who translated it. There will always be those who scoff at the apparent absurdity of angelic visits and divinely guided translation, who belittle the idea of sacred stones

CONCLUSION

being prepared for that purpose, just as Jonathan Hadley did in his paper in 1829. But in matters of faith, it is not the dismissive skeptic or the scornful antagonist whose opinions should rule the day, but those who have embraced the miraculous and felt it transform their soul.

One of those people so transformed was Wilford Woodruff. Woodruff joined the Church because of the words he read in the Book of Mormon. More than a decade of suffering and sacrifice later, in November 1846, Wilford Woodruff reflected on the Book of Mormon. At the time he was an ocean away from the Saints who were then fleeing Illinois into Iowa and preparing to cross the continent, leaning into an uncertain future as they followed Brigham Young out of the United States to find a new home. In his journal, Wilford wrote:

> I . . . have read the Book of Mormon much during the Last twelve years of my life and my soul delighteth much in its words, teaching, and prophesyings. And in its plainness. I rejoice in the goodness and mercy of the God of Israel in preserving the precious Book of Mormon and bringing it to light in our day and generation. It teaches the honest and humble mind the great things of God that were performed in the land of promise, now called America, in ancient days and also the great things of God that are nigh even at the doors. . . . The commencement of this great work and dispensation was like a grain of mustard seed, even small. The plates containing the Book of Mormon were revealed to Joseph Smith and delivered unto him by an angel of God in the month of September, 1827, and translated through the Urim and Thummim into the English language by Joseph Smith, the Prophet, Seer and Revelator."[2]

For Wilford Woodruff, the Book of Mormon was a miracle, a life-changing, world-altering miracle. For him and millions of believers who have since embraced the Book of Mormon, the existence of the book and Joseph Smith's translation of it stand as miracles, however the translation actually

CONCLUSION

occurred. The Book of Mormon stands as its own testament to what Joseph Smith declared publicly: "Through the medium of the Urim and Thummim I translated the record by the gift and power of God."[3]

FURTHER READING

The Church of Jesus Christ of Latter-day Saints. "Book of Mormon Translation." Gospel Topics Essays. https://www.churchofjesuschrist.org/study/manual/gospel-topics-essays/book-of-mormon-translation?lang=eng.

MacKay, Michael Hubbard, and Gerrit J. Dirkmaat. *From Darkness unto Light: Joseph Smith's Translation and Publication of the Book of Mormon*. Provo, UT: Religious Studies Center; Salt Lake City: Deseret Book, 2015.

MacKay, Michael Hubbard, Gerrit J. Dirkmaat, Grant Underwood, Robert J. Woodford, and William G. Hartley, eds. *Documents, Volume 1: July 1828–June 1831*. Vol. 1 of the Documents series of *The Joseph Smith Papers*. Edited by Dean C. Jessee, Ronald K. Esplin, Richard Lyman Bushman, and Matthew J. Grow. Salt Lake City: Church Historian's Press, 2013.

Skousen, Royal. "How Joseph Smith Translated the Book of Mormon." *Journal of Book of Mormon Studies* 7, no. 1 (1997).

Welch, John, ed. "The Miraculous Translation of the Book of Mormon." In *Opening the Heavens: Accounts of Divine Manifestations, 1820–1844*. Provo, UT: BYU Press, 2005.

MacKay, Michael Hubbard, and Nicholas J. Frederick. *Joseph Smith's Seer Stones*. Salt Lake City: Deseret Book, 2016.

Brown, Samuel Morris. *Joseph Smith's Translation: The Words and Worlds of Early Mormonism*. Oxford: Oxford University Press, 2020.

Gardner, Brandt A. *The Gift and Power: Translating the Book of Mormon*. Sandy, UT: Greg A. Kofford Books, 2011.

NOTES

Introduction: Of Men and Miracles

1. *Wayne Sentinel*, June 26, 1829.
2. "Gold Bible," *Palmyra Freeman*, August 11, 1829.
3. Joseph Smith to John Wentworth, *Times and Seasons*, March 1, 1842.

Chapter 1: Visions and Failures

1. The First Presidency and Council of the Twelve Apostles of The Church of Jesus Christ of Latter-day Saints, "The Restoration of the Fulness of the Gospel of Jesus Christ: A Bicentennial Proclamation to the World," ChurchofJesusChrist.org. This proclamation was read by President Russell M. Nelson as part of his message at the 190th Annual General Conference, on April 5, 2020, in Salt Lake City.
2. Brigham Young, discourse, March 25, 1855, Papers of George D. Watt, MS 4534, Church History Library, Salt Lake City.
3. Young, discourse, March 25, 1855.
4. Joseph Smith, history, 1832, 4, Church History Library, available at "History, circa Summer 1832," The Joseph Smith Papers, https://www.josephsmithpapers.org/paper-summary/history-circa-summer-1832/1.
5. "History Drafts, 1838–circa 1841," in Karen Lynn Davidson, David J. Whittaker, Mark Ashurst-McGee, and Richard L. Jensen, eds., *Histories, Volume 1: Joseph Smith Histories, 1832–1844*, vol. 1 of the Histories series of *The Joseph Smith Papers*, ed. Dean C. Jessee, Ronald K. Esplin, and Richard Lyman Bushman (Salt Lake City: Church Historian's Press, 2012), 220.
6. Historian Daniel Vickers provided this definition of the ideal of competency: "[It] connoted the possession of sufficient property to absorb the labors of a given family while providing it with something more than a mere subsistence. It meant, in brief, a degree of comfortable independence." The Smiths never reached this economic or social status while living in Palmyra. Daniel Vickers, "Competency and Competition: Economic Culture in Early America," *The William and Mary Quarterly* 47, no. 1 (January 1990): 3.
7. Lucy Mack Smith, history, 1845 manuscript, 69, Church History Library, available at "Lucy Mack Smith, History, 1845," The Joseph

NOTES

Smith Papers, https://www.josephsmithpapers.org/paper-summary/lucy-mack-smith-history-1845/354.

8. Smith, history, 1832, 4.
9. "Church History," *Times and Seasons*, March 1, 1842, available at The Joseph Smith Papers, https://www.josephsmithpapers.org/paper-summary/times-and-seasons-1-march-1842/5.
10. Smith, history, 1832, 4.
11. Smith, history, 1832, 4.
12. Joseph Smith, "Journal, 1835–1836," 25 (November 9, 1836), The Joseph Smith Papers, https://www.josephsmithpapers.org/paper-summary/journal-1835-1836/26.
13. "History, 1838–1856, volume A-1 [23 December 1805–30 August 1834]," 5, The Joseph Smith Papers, https://www.josephsmithpapers.org/paper-summary/history-1838-1856-volume-a-1-23-december-1805-30-august-1834/1.
14. "History, 1838–1856, volume A-1," 5.
15. "History, 1838–1856, volume A-1," 6.
16. Lucy Mack Smith, history, 1845 manuscript, 90.
17. Smith, "Journal, 1835–1836," 25 (November 9, 1836); "History, 1834–1836," 122, The Joseph Smith Papers, https://www.josephsmithpapers.org/paper-summary/history-1834-1836/1.
18. "History, circa June 1839–circa 1841 [Draft 2]," 24, The Joseph Smith Papers, https://www.josephsmithpapers.org/paper-summary/history-circa-june-1839-circa-1841-draft-2/30.
19. See Steven C. Harper, "The Probation of a Teenage Seer: Joseph Smith's Early Experiences with Moroni," in *The Coming Forth of the Book of Mormon: A Marvelous Work and a Wonder*, ed. Dennis L. Largey, Andrew H. Hedges, John Hilton III, and Kerry Hull (Provo, UT: Religious Studies Center; Salt Lake City: Deseret Book, 2015), 33–35. Lucy Mack Smith wrote, "The thought flashed across his mind that there might be something more in the box that might would be a benefit to him in a pecuniary point of view." Lucy Mack Smith, history, 1844–1845, p. [2], bk. 4, Church History Library, available at "Lucy Mack Smith, History, 1844–1845," The Joseph Smith Papers, https://www.josephsmithpapers.org/paper-summary/lucy-mack-smith-history-1844-1845/1.
20. Oliver Cowdery to William W. Phelps, October 1835, copied into volume A-1 of the manuscript history; "History, 1834–1836," 93.
21. Smith, history, 1832, 4; spelling modernized.
22. Smith, history, 1832, 4; spelling modernized. Oliver Cowdery softened the failure to the readers of his letter: "In this, which occasioned a failure to obtain, at that time, the record, do not understand me to attach blame to our brother: he was young, and his mind easily turned from correct principles, unless he could be favored with a certain round of experience." Cowdery to Phelps, October 1835; spelling modernized.
23. Smith, history, 1832, 4.
24. "History, 1838–1856, volume A-1," 7.

NOTES

Chapter 2: Marrying Emma and Obtaining the Plates

1. For a thorough discussion of Emma and Joseph's courtship, marriage, and relationship, see Jennifer Reeder, *First: The Life and Faith of Emma Smith* (Salt Lake City: Deseret Book, 2021).
2. Lucy Mack Smith, history, 1845 manuscript, 97, Church History Library, Salt Lake City, available at "Lucy Mack Smith, History, 1845," The Joseph Smith Papers, https://www.josephsmithpapers.org/paper-summary/lucy-mack-smith-history-1845/1.
3. Isaac Hale, affidavit, March 20, 1834, printed in Eber Howe, *Mormonism Unvailed* (Painesville, OH, 1834), 263.
4. Joseph Smith III, "Last Testimony of Sister Emma," *Saints' Herald*, October 1, 1879, 289–90.
5. Smith III, "Last Testimony of Sister Emma," 289–90. This is not to say that they did not come to intensely love one another over the course of their marriage. That they did so seems quite clear in the documentary record.
6. Lucy Mack Smith, history, 1844–1845, p. [5], bk. 5, Church History Library; punctuation modernized; available at "Lucy Mack Smith, History, 1844–1845," The Joseph Smith Papers, https://www.josephsmithpapers.org/paper-summary/lucy-mack-smith-history-1844-1845/1.
7. Lucy Mack Smith, history, 1845 manuscript, 104.
8. "History, circa June 1839–circa 1841 [Draft 2]," 8, The Joseph Smith Papers, https://www.josephsmithpapers.org/paper-summary/history-circa-june-1839-circa-1841-draft-2/10.
9. Lucy Mack Smith, history, 1845 manuscript, 113.
10. Lucy Mack Smith, history, 1844–1845, p. [11], bk. 5.

Chapter 3: Early Translation with Emma and Martin, 1828

1. For more on Joseph's efforts to hide the plates, see Andrew Hedges, "All My Endeavors to Preserve Them": Protecting the Plates in Palmyra, 22 September–December 1827," *Journal of Book of Mormon Studies* 8, no. 2, (1999).
2. "Old Town Record, 1793–1870," 221, Township Office, Palmyra, New York, Family History Library, Salt Lake City.
3. Eber Howe, *Mormonism Unvailed* (Painesville, OH, 1834), 263–64.
4. Karen Lynn Davidson, David J. Whittaker, Mark Ashurst-McGee, and Richard L. Jensen, eds., *Histories, Volume 1: Joseph Smith Histories, 1832–1844*, vol. 1 of the Histories series of *The Joseph Smith Papers*, ed. Dean C. Jessee, Ronald K. Esplin, and Richard Lyman Bushman (Salt Lake City: Church Historian's Press, 2012), 238; "History, 1838–1856, volume A-1 [23 December 1805–30 August 1834]," 8, The Joseph Smith Papers, https://www.josephsmithpapers.org/paper-summary/history-1838-1856-volume-a-1-23-december-1805-30-august-1834/1.
5. Lucy Mack Smith, history, 1844–1845, p. [6], bk. 6, Church History

NOTES

Library, Salt Lake City, available at "Lucy Mack Smith, History, 1844–1845," The Joseph Smith Papers, https://www.josephsmith papers.org/paper-summary/lucy-mack-smith-history-1844-1845/1.

6. Davidson and others, eds., *Histories, Volume 1*, 238. All was eventually crossed out and not used in the Coray copy of the published version. "History, 1838–1856, volume A-1," 9.

7. Michael Hubbard MacKay, Robin Jensen, and Gerrit Dirkmaat, "The 'Caractors' Document: New Light on an Early Transcription of the Book of Mormon Characters," *Mormon Historical Studies* 14, no. 1 (Spring 2013); "History, 1838–1856, volume A-1," 9; spelling modernized.

8. Michael Hubbard MacKay, "'Git them Translated': Joseph Smith and the Translation of the Characters on the Gold Plates," in *Approaching Antiquity: Joseph Smith and the Ancient World*, ed. Lincoln Blumel, Matthew Grey, and Andrew Hedges (Provo, UT: Religious Studies Center; Salt Lake City: Deseret Book, 2015), 83–118.

9. MacKay, "Git them Translated," 82, 102; spelling modernized.

10. "History, 1838–1856, volume A-1," 9; spelling modernized.

11. For a detailed account of the scholars Martin visited on his journey to the Eastern cities, see Michael Hubbard MacKay and Gerrit J. Dirkmaat, *From Darkness unto Light: Joseph Smith's Translation and Publication of the Book of Mormon* (Provo, UT: Religious Studies Center; Salt Lake City: Deseret Book, 2015), 39–59. See also Richard E. Bennett, "'Read This I Pray Thee': Martin Harris and the Three Wise Men of the East," *Journal of Mormon History* 36, no. 1 (Winter 2010): 178–216.

12. Davidson and others, eds., *Histories, Volume 1*, 240; "History, 1838–1856, volume A-1," 9.

13. Joseph Smith, history, 1832, 5, Church History Library; spelling as in original; available at "History, circa Summer 1832," The Joseph Smith Papers, https://www.josephsmithpapers.org/paper-summary/history-circa-summer-1832/5.

14. Joseph Knight Sr., history, 4.

15. Joseph Smith III, "Last Testimony of Sister Emma," *Saints' Herald*, October 1, 1879, 289–90.

16. "Now the first that my husband translated was translated by the use of the Urim and Thummim, and that was the part that Martin Harris lost." Emma Smith to Emma Pilgrim, March 27, 1870, Community of Christ Library and Archives, Independence, MO.

17. Martin Harris, interview with Simon Smith, as copied in letter to Joseph Smith III, December 29, 1880, Miscellaneous Letters and Papers, Community of Christ Library and Archives.

18. Martin Harris, quoted in Simon Smith, "To the Editor," *Saints' Herald*, May 24, 1884, 324.

19. John Clark, *Gleanings by the Way* (Philadelphia: W. J. & J. K. Simon, for Robert Carter, 1842), 222–24, 254.

20. Lucy Mack Smith, history, 1844–1845, p. [8], bk. 6.

NOTES

21. Lucy Mack Smith, history, 1844–1845, p. [8], bk. 6.
22. "She told Mr Dikes that if he would contrive to get the egyptian characters out of Martins possession of and hire a room in Palmira & take transcribe them accurately and bring her the transcripts that she would give him her daug[h]ter Lucy to wife Mr Dikes readily agreed to this and sufice it to say he succeeded to the woman's satisfaction and received the promised reward." Lucy Mack Smith, history, 1844–1845, p. [8], bk. 6; spelling as in original.
23. Lucy Mack Smith, history, 1844–1845, p. [9], bk. 6.
24. Davidson and others, eds., *Histories, Volume 1*, 15; Smith, history, 1832, 5.
25. Fred C. Collier and William S. Harwell, eds., *Kirtland Council Minute Book* (Salt Lake City: Collier's Publishing, 1996), 21; "Minutes, 12 February 1834," 28, The Joseph Smith Papers, https://www.josephsmithpapers.org/paper-summary/minutes-12-february-1834/2.
26. *Deseret Evening News*, December 13, 1881.
27. *Book of Mormon* (Palmyra, NY: E.B. Grandin, 1830), iii–iv.
28. Simon Smith, "To the Editor," *Saints' Herald*, May 24, 1884, 324.
29. "History, 1838–1856, volume A-1," 9.
30. "History, circa June–October 1839 [Draft 1]," [5], The Joseph Smith Papers, https://www.josephsmithpapers.org/paper-summary/history-circa-june-october-1839-draft-1/5.
31. Joseph Smith, history, 1832, [6]; spelling as in original.
32. Davidson and others, eds., *Histories, Volume 1*, 244.

Chapter 4: Loss Precedes the Miracle

1. Karen Lynn Davidson, David J. Whittaker, Mark Ashurst-McGee, and Richard L. Jensen, eds., *Histories, Volume 1: Joseph Smith Histories, 1832–1844*, vol. 1 of the Histories series of *The Joseph Smith Papers*, ed. Dean C. Jessee, Ronald K. Esplin, and Richard Lyman Bushman (Salt Lake City: Church Historian's Press, 2012), 244.
2. Book of Mormon (NY: E. B. Grandin, 1830), preface.
3. Lucy Mack Smith, history, 1844–1845, p. 2, bk. 7, Church History Library, Salt Lake City; available at "Lucy Mack Smith, History, 1844–1845," The Joseph Smith Papers, https://www.josephsmithpapers.org/paper-summary/lucy-mack-smith-history-1844-1845/1.
4. Lucy Mack Smith, history, 1844–1845, p. 2, bk. 7.
5. Lucy Mack Smith, history, 1844–1845, p. 6, bk. 7.
6. Lucy Mack Smith, history, 1844–1845, p. 7, bk. 7.
7. "History, circa June–October 1839 [Draft 1]," [24], The Joseph Smith Papers, https://www.josephsmithpapers.org/paper-summary/history-circa-june-october-1839-draft-1/24.
8. "Revelation, July 1828 [D&C 3]," 1, The Joseph Smith Papers, https://www.josephsmithpapers.org/paper-summary/revelation-july-1828-dc-3/1.
9. Lucy Mack Smith, history, 1844–1845, pp. 7–8, bk. 7; *JSP, Histories, vol. 1*, 252. 1.

NOTES

10. Lucy Mack Smith, history, 1844–1845, pp. 7–8, bk. 7; spelling modernized.
11. Lucy Mack Smith, history, 1844–1845, p. 11, bk. 7. 8
12. Lucy Mack Smith, history, 1844–1845, pp. 5–7, bk. 12.
13. Joseph Knight Sr., history, 5; spelling modernized.
14. Davidson and others, eds., *Histories, Volume 1*, 16.
15. "Testimony of Martin Harris," September 4, 1870, Edward Stevenson Collection, Church History Library; spelling and grammar modernized.
16. Lucy Mack Smith, history, 1845, pp. [7–8], bk. 8; Peter Ingersoll statement in Eber Howe, *Mormonism Unvailed* (Painesville, OH, 1834), 236.
17. See "Joseph Rogers' Statement," in *Startling Revelations! Naked Truths about Mormonism*, ed. Arthur B. Deming (Oakland, CA: n.p., 1888), 1. Edward Stevenson records the only brief account we have of him from Martin Harris. After hearing of the threat of a lawsuit, Harris stated, "So I went from Waterloo 25 mls South East of Palmyra to Rogerses in Suscotua [?] Co N.Y. & to harmony Pensylvania 125 & found Joseph. Rogers unknown to me had agreed to give my wife 100 Dollars if it was not A Deseption & had Whet his Nife to cut the covering of the Plates as the Lord had forbid Joseph exhibiting them openly." "Testimony of Martin Harris," September 4, 1870.
18. "Mormonism," *Tiffany's Monthly*, August 1859, 166; Howe, *Mormonism Unvailed*, 264.
19. "Mormonism," *Kansas City Daily Journal*, June 1, 1881.
20. Davidson and others, eds., *Histories, Volume 1*, 16; "History, circa Summer 1832," [6], The Joseph Smith Papers, https://www.josephsmithpapers.org/paper-summary/history-circa-summer-1832/6.
21. "Mormonism," *Kansas City Daily Journal*, June 1, 1881; "Report of Elders Orson Pratt and Joseph F. Smith," *Millennial Star* 40 (December 9, 1878): 771–74.

Chapter 5: Finishing the Work

1. Michael Hubbard MacKay, Gerrit J. Dirkmaat, Grant Underwood, Robert J. Woodford, and William C. Hartley, eds., *Documents, Volume 1: July 1828–June 1831*, vol. 1 of the Documents series of *The Joseph Smith Papers*, ed. Dean C. Jessee, Ronald K. Esplin, Richard Lyman Bushman, and Matthew J. Grow (Salt Lake City: Church Historian's Press, 2013), 27–33; spelling modernized.
2. Karen Lynn Davidson, David J. Whittaker, Mark Ashurst-McGee, and Richard L. Jensen, eds., *Histories, Volume 1: Joseph Smith Histories, 1832–1844*, vol. 1 of the Histories series of *The Joseph Smith Papers*, ed. Dean C. Jessee, Ronald K. Esplin, and Richard Lyman Bushman (Salt Lake City: Church Historian's Press, 2012), 276.
3. James H. Hart, "About the Book of Mormon," *Deseret News*, April 9, 1884, 190.
4. MacKay and others, eds., *Documents, Volume 1*, 35–37; "Book of

NOTES

Commandments, 1833," 16, The Joseph Smith Papers, https://www.josephsmithpapers.org/paper-summary/book-of-commandments-1833/20.

5. MacKay and others, eds., *Documents, Volume 1*, 36; "Book of Commandments, 1833," 16.

6. The earliest copy of this revelation states that the "spirt by which Moses brought the children of Israel through the red sea on dry ground." Or, like the "gift of working with the sprout" or rod. MacKay and others, eds., *Documents, Volume 1*, 45; "Revelation, April 1829–B [D&C 8]," 13, The Joseph Smith Papers, https://www.josephsmithpapers.org/paper-summary/revelation-april-1829-b-dc-8/2.

7. MacKay and others, eds., *Documents, Volume 1*, 47–48; "Account of John, April 1829–C [D&C 7]," 13, The Joseph Smith Papers, https://www.josephsmithpapers.org/paper-summary/account-of-john-april-1829-c-dc-7/1.

8. Oliver Cowdery to William W. Phelps, September 7, 1834, *Latter Day Saints' Messenger and Advocate* 1 (October 1834): 14.

9. Oliver Cowdery, "Dear Brother," *Latter Day Saints' Messenger and Advocate* 1 (October 1834): 15; Lucy Mack Smith, history, 1844–1845, p. 4, bk. 8, Church History Library, Salt Lake City, available at "Lucy Mack Smith, History, 1844–1845," The Joseph Smith Papers, https://www.josephsmithpapers.org/paper-summary/lucy-mack-smith-history-1844-1845/1.

10. The First Presidency and Council of the Twelve Apostles of The Church of Jesus Christ of Latter-day Saints, "The Restoration of the Fulness of the Gospel of Jesus Christ: A Bicentennial Proclamation to the World," April 5, 2020, ChurchofJesusChrist.org.

    In 2019, President Russell M. Nelson similarly explained that there "came a succession of visits from heavenly messengers, including Moroni, John the Baptist, and the early Apostles Peter, James, and John. Others followed, including Moses, Elias, and Elijah. Each brought divine authority to bless God's children on the earth once again." "Closing Remarks," general conference, October 2019, https://www.churchofjesuschrist.org/study/general-conference/2019/10/57nelson?lang=eng; see also Michael Hubbard Mackay, "Event or Process? How 'the Chamber of Old Father Whitmer' Helps Us Understand Priesthood Restoration," *BYU Studies Quarterly* 60, no. 1 (2021): 73–101; MacKay and others, eds., *Documents, Volume 1*, xxxvii–xxxviii; "Joseph Smith Documents Dating through June 1831," The Joseph Smith Papers, https://www.josephsmithpapers.org/intro/introduction-to-documents-volume-1-july-1828-june-1831?p=1&highlight=introduction to documents volume 1.

11. "History, 1838–1856, volume A-1 [23 December 1805–30 August 1834]," 8, The Joseph Smith Papers, https://www.josephsmithpapers.org/paper-summary/history-1838-1856-volume-a-1-23-december-1805-30-august-1834/1.

12. MacKay and others, eds., *Documents, Volume 1*, 38–44; "Revelation,

NOTES

Spring 1829 [D&C 10]," 26, The Joseph Smith Papers, https://www.josephsmithpapers.org/paper-summary/revelation-spring-1829-dc-10/5.

13. Davidson and others, eds., *Histories, Volume 1*, 304.
14. Davidson and others, eds., *Histories, Volume 1*, 308.
15. Lucy Mack Smith, history, 1845 manuscript, 151, Church History Library, available at "Lucy Mack Smith, History, 1845," The Joseph Smith Papers, https://www.josephsmithpapers.org/paper-summary/lucy-mack-smith-history-1845/158.
16. *Deseret Evening News*, November 16, 1878; Lucy Mack Smith, history, 1844–1845, p. [10], bk. 8. "His answer was that he should give himself no trouble about but hasten her to waterloo and after he arrived a[t] Mr. Whitmore's house if he would repair immediately to the garden he would receive the plates from the hand of an angel to whose charge they must be committed for their safety."
17. "Report of Elders Orson Pratt and Joseph F. Smith," *Millennial Star*, December 9, 1878, 772–73.
18. Davidson and others, eds., *Histories, Volume 1*, 312–14; "History, circa June 1839–circa 1841 [Draft 2]," 23, The Joseph Smith Papers, https://www.josephsmithpapers.org/paper-summary/history-circa-june-1839-circa-1841-draft-2/29.
19. "Doctrine and Covenants, 1835," 169, The Joseph Smith Papers, https://www.josephsmithpapers.org/paper-summary/doctrine-and-covenants-1835/1.
20. "Doctrine and Covenants, 1835," 172.
21. MacKay and others, eds., *Documents, Volume 1*, 368–77; "Appendix 3: "Articles of the Church of Christ," June 1829," p. [1], The Joseph Smith Papers, https://www.josephsmithpapers.org/paper-summary/appendix-3-articles-of-the-church-of-christ-june-1829/1.
22. Lucy Mack Smith, history, 1844–1845, p. [11], bk. 8.
23. "History, 1838–1856, volume A-1 [23 December 1805–30 August 1834]," 25; see also William E. McLellin, journal, June–August 1831, William E. McLellin, Papers, Church History Library; "History, circa June 1839–circa 1841 [Draft 2]," 25, The Joseph Smith Papers, https://www.josephsmithpapers.org/paper-summary/history-circa-june-1839-circa-1841-draft-2/31.
24. "History, 1838–1856, volume A-1 [23 December 1805–30 August 1834]," 25.
25. "Appendix 4: Testimony of Three Witnesses, Late June 1829," [589], The Joseph Smith Papers, https://www.josephsmithpapers.org/paper-summary/appendix-4-testimony-of-three-witnesses-late-june-1829/1.
26. "Report of Elders Orson Pratt and Joseph F. Smith," *Deseret News*, November 16, 1878.
27. "Testimony of Three Witnesses, Late June 1829," [589].
28. "Testimony of Three Witnesses, Late June 1829," [589].
29. "Testimony of Three Witnesses, Late June 1829," [589].

NOTES

30. *Deseret News*, August 6, 1878.
31. "Appendix 5: Testimony of Eight Witnesses, Late June 1829," [590], The Joseph Smith Papers, https://www.josephsmithpapers.org/paper-summary/appendix-5-testimony-of-eight-witnesses-late-june-1829/1.
32. For more on the publication of the Book of Mormon, see Gerrit Dirkmaat and Michael Hubbard MacKay, "Joseph Smith's Negotiations to Publish the Book of Mormon," in *The Coming Forth of the Book of Mormon: 44th Annual Brigham Young University Sidney B. Sperry Symposium* (Provo, UT: Religious Studies Center, Brigham Young University, 2015).

Chapter 6: How Did Joseph Translate the Book of Mormon?

1. Daniel Walker Howe, *What Hath God Wrought: The Transformation of America, 1815–1848*, The Oxford History of the United States (New York: Oxford University Press, 2007), 314.
2. "History, circa Summer 1832," 5, The Joseph Smith Papers, https://www.josephsmithpapers.org/paper-summary/history-circa-summer-1832/1.
3. Edmund C. Briggs, "A Visit to Nauvoo in 1856," *Journal of History* 9 (October 1916): 454.
4. "History, 1838–1856, volume A-1 [23 December 1805–30 August 1834]," 5, The Joseph Smith Papers, https://www.josephsmithpapers.org/paper-summary/history-1838-1856-volume-a-1-23-december-1805-30-august-1834/5; Joseph Smith, "Journal, 1835–1836," 26, The Joseph Smith Papers, https://www.josephsmithpapers.org/paper-summary/journal-1835-1836/27.
5. "History, circa Summer 1832," 5.
6. See the first published version of Joseph Smith's history, *Times and Seasons*, March 1, 1842, https://www.josephsmithpapers.org/paper-summary/times-and-seasons-1-march-1842/5.
7. It is possible that the device given to the brother of Jared and the one used by Mosiah are the same device, but the Book of Mormon does not say this expressly. For a larger discussion on these stones, see Michael Hubbard MacKay and Nicholas J. Frederick, *Joseph Smith's Seer Stones* (Salt Lake City: Deseret Book, 2016).
8. Joseph Knight Sr., history, Church History Library, Salt Lake City, 4; spelling and grammar modernized.
9. David Whitmer, *An Address to All Believers in Christ* (Richmond, MO: By the author, 1887), 12.
10. Christian Goodwillie, "Shaker Richard McNemar: The Earliest Book of Mormon Reviewer," *Journal of Mormon History* 37, no. 2 (Spring 2011): 143.
11. "History of the Mormonites," *The Evangelist*, June 1, 1841.
12. Joel Tiffany, "Mormonism," *Tiffany's Monthly*, August 1859, 165.
13. "One of the Three Witnesses," *Deseret Evening News*, December 13, 1881.

NOTES

14. See the introduction, p. 1 herein.
15. Jonathan Hadley, "Golden Bible," *Palmyra Freeman,* August 11, 1829.
16. Hadley, "Golden Bible."
17. Joseph Smith, "Church History," *Times and Seasons,* March 1, 1842.
18. Hadley, "Golden Bible."
19. Emma Smith to Emma Pilgrim, March 27, 1870, in John T. Clark, "Translation of Nephite Records," *Return* (Davis City, IA), July 15, 1895, 2.
20. *Deseret Evening News,* December 13, 1881, 4.
21. George A. Smith Papers, box 174, folder 26, Manuscripts Division, Marriott Library, University of Utah, Salt Lake City.
22. According to Brigham Young, Joseph was actually able to find the sacred stone by looking at another stone: "He saw it while looking in another seers stone which a person had. He went right to the spot & dug & found it." Wilford Woodruff, journal, September 11, 1859, Church History Library.
23. Woodruff, journal, March 18, 1888.
24. Woodruff, journal, May 18, 1888.
25. Russell M. Nelson, "A Treasured Testament," *Ensign,* July 1993, 61–63, quoting David Whitmer, *An Address to All Believers in Christ* (Richmond, Mo.: n.p., 1887), 12.
26. Neal A. Maxwell, "By the Gift and Power of God," *Ensign,* January 1997, 36–41
27. Michael Hubbard MacKay, Gerrit J. Dirkmaat, Grant Underwood, Robert J. Woodford, and William G. Hartley, eds, *Documents, Volume 1: July 1828–June 1831,* vol. 1 of the Documents series of *The Joseph Smith Papers,* ed. Dean C. Jessee, Ronald K. Esplin, Richard Lyman Bushman, and Matthew J. Grow (Salt Lake City: Church Historian's Press, 2013), xxix–xxxii.
28. "How Did Joseph Smith Translate the Book of Mormon?" *New Era,* April 2020.
29. *Foundations of the Restoration Teacher Material* (Salt Lake City: The Church of Jesus Christ of Latter-day Saints, 2020), 40.
30. Dieter F. Uchtdorf, Facebook post, June 21, 2016.
31. "The Book of Mormon Is Tangible Evidence of the Restoration" (video), The Church of Jesus Christ of Latter-day Saints, https://www.churchofjesuschrist.org/media/video/2020-05-0290-the-book-of-mormon-is-tangible-evidence-of-the-restoration?lang=eng.

Chapter 7: Important Questions and Possible Answers

1. For an in-depth examination of the stones Joseph used during his seership, see Michael Hubbard MacKay and Nicholas J. Frederick, *Joseph Smith's Seer Stones* (Salt Lake City: Deseret Book, 2016).
2. "History, circa June–October 1839 [Draft 1]," [5], The Joseph Smith Papers, https://www.josephsmithpapers.org/paper-summary/history-circa-june-october-1839-draft-1/5.

NOTES

3. While Doctrine and Covenants 17 does use the term "Urim and Thummim," the earliest surviving version of this revelation was copied in late 1834 at the earliest. See "Revelation, June 1829–E [D&C 17]," 119, The Joseph Smith Papers, https://www.josephsmithpapers.org/paper-summary/revelation-june-1829-e-dc-17/1. Though the revelation was first received in June 1829, the early copies of it did not survive, and it seems that when the revelation was edited to appear in the 1835 Doctrine and Covenants (it had not been included in the 1833 Book of Commandments), the term "Urim and Thummim" was inserted, much like it was in the revelation that is now known as Doctrine and Covenants 10. See Michael Hubbard MacKay, Gerrit J. Dirkmaat, Grant Underwood, Robert J. Woodford, and William G. Hartley, eds, *Documents, Volume 1: July 1828–June 1831,* vol. 1 of the Documents series of *The Joseph Smith Papers,* ed. Dean C. Jessee, Ronald K Esplin, Richard Lyman Bushman, and Matthew J. Grow (Salt Lake City: Church Historian's Press, 2013), 82; "Revelation, Spring 1829 [D&C 10]," 22, The Joseph Smith Papers, https://www.josephsmithpapers.org/paper-summary/revelation-spring-1829-dc-10/1.
4. *Deseret Evening News,* December 13, 1881.
5. "Mormonism," *Tiffany,* August 1859, 163–70.
6. Lucy Mack Smith, history, 1844–1845, 7, Church History Library, Salt Lake City, available at "Lucy Mack Smith, History, 1844–1845," The Joseph Smith Papers, https://www.josephsmithpapers.org/paper-summary/lucy-mack-smith-history-1844-1845/1; spelling modernized.
7. Jesse Smith to Hyrum Smith, June 17, 1829, Letter Book 2, MS 155, Church History Library; spelling modernized. There had been no published descriptions of Joseph's find or the translation at this early date. Jesse Smith was not simply parroting back what he had read in a newspaper but directly responding with the terminology his nephew Hyrum had used.
8. "History, circa Summer 1832," 5, The Joseph Smith Papers, https://www.josephsmithpapers.org/paper-summary/history-circa-summer-1832/5. In August 1829, before any accounts of translation had been published to borrow information from, printer Jonathan Hadley recited the translation process as Joseph had described it to him. He explained that when Joseph found the plates, it was "together with a huge pair of Spectacles! . . . By placing the Spectacles in a hat, and looking into it, Smith could (he said so, at least,) interpret these characters." "Gold Bible," *Palmyra Freeman,* August 11, 1829.
9. Titus Strong, *The Scholar's Guide to the History of the Bible* (Greenfield, Clark & Tyler, 1822), 54.
10. "The Book of Mormon," *The Evening and the Morning Star,* January 1833, 2.
11. Joseph Smith, journal, November 9, 1835, MS 155, Church History Library.

NOTES

12. "History, circa Summer 1832," 5.
13. Joseph Smith, journal, November 9, 1835.
14. "Answers to Questions," *Elders' Journal*, July 1835.
15. "Church History," *Times and Seasons*, March 1, 1842.
16. "History of Joseph Smith," *Times and Seasons*, April 15, 1842.
17. *Book of Commandments*, 1830, chap. 9, v. 1, p. 22.
18. Doctrine and Covenants, 1835, 36:1, p. 163; emphasis added.
19. School of the Prophets Salt Lake City Records, Minutes, January 17, 1871, CR 390 6, Church History Library.
20. "Two Days' Meeting at Brigham City, June 27 and 28, 1874," *Millennial Star*, August 11, 1874, 498–99. See Richard Turley, Robin S. Jensen, and Mark Ashurst-McGee, "Joseph the Seer," Ensign, October 2015, https://www.churchofjesuschrist.org/study/ensign/2015/10/joseph-the-seer?lang=eng.
21. James R. B. Van Cleave to Joseph Smith III, September 29, 1878, Community of Christ Library Archives, Independence, MO; see Doctrine and Covenants 34.
22. Edward Stevenson, *Reminiscences of Joseph, The Prophet,* (Salt Lake City, 1893), 6.
23. Wilford Woodruff, journal, December 27, 1841, Church History Library. For more information on the seer stones Joseph Smith possessed, see MacKay and Frederick, *Joseph Smith's Seer Stones*.
24. Woodruff, journal, February 19, 1842; spelling and punctuation modernized.
25. Woodruff, journal, February 19, 1842; spelling and punctuation modernized.
26. Reuben Miller, journal, October 21, 1848; spelling and grammar modernized.
27. See Royal Skousen, "How Joseph Smith Translated the Book of Mormon," *Journal of Book of Mormon Studies* 7, no. 1 (1997).
28. For the deep articulation of this argument, see Samuel Brown, *Joseph Smith's Translation: The Words and Worlds of Early Mormonism* (Oxford: Oxford University Press, 2020). Brandt Gardner, another Latter-day Saint scholar, also challenges the Skousen theory of word-for-word dictation, but for different reasons. In any case, all of these men still hold to the miraculous nature of the translation despite their differences about how it occurred. See Brandt A. Gardner, *The Gift and Power: Translating the Book of Mormon* (Sandy, UT: Greg A. Kofford Books, 2011).
29. "Book of Mormon Translation," Gospel Topics Essays, The Church of Jesus Christ of Latter-day Saints, https://www.churchofjesuschrist.org/study/manual/gospel-topics-essays/book-of-mormon-translation?lang=eng.
30. Royal Skousen, "Translating the Book of Mormon: Evidence from the Original Manuscript," in *Book of Mormon Authorship Revisited: The Evidence for Ancient Origins*, ed. Noel B. Reynolds (Provo, UT: Foundation for Ancient Research and Mormon Studies, 1997).

NOTES

31. Joseph Smith III, "Last Testimony of Sister Emma," *Saints' Herald*, October 1, 1879, 289–90; emphasis added.
32. See *Painesville Telegraph*, February 15, 1831; February 22, 1831; and March 15, 1831, for examples.
33. Joseph Smith, journal, April 30, 1834.
34. Eber Howe, *Mormonism Unvailed* (Painesville, OH, 1834), 270–71.
35. John A. Clark, *Gleanings by the Way* (Philadelphia: W. J. & J. K. Simon, 1842), 230.
36. One very late reminiscent account published in 1880 by a Harmony, Pennsylvania, resident also claimed that there were blankets nailed to the walls to prevent the scribes from seeing what was going on, but this is directly contradicted by Emma Smith's assertion that nothing was between them in Harmony while Joseph translated and she wrote. "The Early Mormons. Joe Smith Operates at Susquehanna," *Binghamton Republican*, July 29, 1880
37. "The Book of Mormon," *Chicago Tribune*, December 17, 1885.
38. Lucy Mack Smith, *History*, 117.
39. "Letter from W. H. Kelley," *Saints' Herald*, March 1, 1882.
40. David Whitmer, *An Address to All Believers in Christ* (Richmond, MO, 1887), 30.

Conclusion

1. Whitmer, *An Address to All Believers in Christ*, 12.
2. Woodruff, journal, November 2, 1846; spelling and punctuation modernized.
3. Joseph Smith to John Wentworth, "Church History," *Times and Seasons*, March 1, 1842.

INDEX

Abraham, 88
Ammon, 64–65
Anthon, Charles, 27, 103–4
Ashurst-McGee, Mark, 76

Baptism, 52, 53
Bible, 87–89, 90–91
Book of Lehi, 29–30, 33–35, 37–41, 45, 53–55, 86
Book of Mormon: publication of, 1–2, 56; impact of, 2–3; as keystone of LDS religion, 3; and Joseph Smith's spiritual progression, 10–11; lost manuscript pages of, 33–35, 37–41, 53–55, 86; possible dictation of, 93–95; missteps in, 94–95; transformation through, 108–10. *See also* Book of Mormon translation; gold plates
Book of Mormon translation: method / process for, 3–4, 5–6, 62–79, 92–93; witnesses of, 7, 8, 108; early, with Emma Smith and Martin Harris, 25–35; timeline of, 36; work on, recommences, 41–43; finishing, 48–61; modern writings on, 76–79; use of seer stones versus Urim and Thummim in, 80–84; without seer stones, 84–92; scribes' testimony regarding use of seer stones in, 95–98;

theories regarding, 96–98; Joseph Smith's possible creative involvement in, 98–99; God's method for, 100; other theories regarding, 101–2; sheet separating Joseph and scribes in, 102–5; need for gold plates in, 105–7. *See also* gold plates; seer stones
Bradish, Luther, 27
Brother of Jared, 63–64, 88
Brown, Samuel, 94, 101

Church of Jesus Christ of Latter-day Saints, The, organization of, 56–57
Clark, John A., 30–31, 104
Cowdery, Oliver, 15, 42, 46–60, 69, 81, 91–92, 94, 102

Davis, William, 101
Dyke, Flanders, 31, 32

First Vision, 9

Gardner, Brant, 102
Gazelem, 65, 66, 74–76, 80–81
God, translation method of, 100
Gold plates: obtaining, 11–17, 20–23, 46; attempts to steal, 23, 26; characters of, 26–27, 28, 30–31, 33–34, 71, 103–4; and translation with Urim and Thummim, 28–29; Martin Harris requests to see, 43–46; moving, 56; witnesses of, 56,

INDEX

57–61, 73; description of, 71–72; and sheet separating Joseph and scribes, 102–5; need for, in Book of Mormon translation, 105–7. *See also* Book of Mormon; Book of Mormon translation
Grandin, Egbert, 1, 70

Hadley, Jonathan, 1–2, 61, 70–72
Hale, Isaac, 18, 19, 20, 25, 34, 48, 55
Harris, Lucy, 31–32, 43, 44
Harris, Martin: and Book of Mormon publication, 1; and early Book of Mormon translation, 26, 27, 30–35, 71; loses Book of Mormon manuscript pages, 33–35, 37–40; requests to see gold plates, 43–46; as Book of Mormon witness, 58–60, 105; on Book of Mormon translation method, 69–70, 73, 74; on seer stones, 81; and sheet separating Joseph and scribes, 102, 103–4
Harris Dyke, Lucy, 31
Hat, in translation process, 28, 66, 67–68, 69–70, 72, 73–74, 76, 77, 78–79, 89, 95, 96–97, 102, 108
Historians, 4–6
Howe, Eber D., 73, 103, 104
Howe, Sophia, 103

Interpreters. *See* seer stones

Jared, brother of, 63–64, 88
Jensen, Robin, 76
Jesus Christ, miracles of, 4–5
Jones, Josiah, 69
Joseph Smith Translation, 87–89, 90–91

Knight, Joseph Sr., 26, 42, 55, 67

Limhi, King, 64–65

Maxwell, Neal A., 76–77
Miracles, 4–6
Missteps, 94–95
Mitchill, Samuel L., 27
Mormonism Unvailed (Howe), 103
Moroni, 12–14, 16, 21, 40
Mosiah, 88

Nelson, Russell M., 76, 78–79

Ostler, Blake, 98

Page, Hiram, 60
Phelps, William W., 83
Poverty, 11–12, 14–15, 17
Pratt, Orson, 86–89
Priesthood, restoration of, 52–53

Restoration, 9–10, 52–53
Revelation(s): given to Joseph Smith, 9–10; for Oliver Cowdery, 48–50; versus translation, 93
Rigdon, Sidney, 104

Schucman, Helen, 99
Scribal anticipation, 94
Seers, 86, 88, 106–7
Seer stones: and Book of Mormon translation, 12–13, 27, 63–66, 67–70, 72, 73–79, 80–84, 108; translation without, 84–92; translation witnesses' testimony regarding, 95–98
Sheet, separating Joseph and scribes, 102–5
Skousen, Royal, 93–94, 96, 98–99, 101
Smith, Alvin, 13
Smith, Emma Hale: courtship with Joseph, 18; marriage of, 18–20; financial situation of, 25; and Book of Mormon translation, 25–27, 28–30, 63; as Book of Mormon witness, 28–29, 105; health issues of, 38–39; and renewed

INDEX

translation of Book of Mormon, 41; on Joseph's writing abilities, 63; on Book of Mormon translation method, 66–67, 73, 74; and sheet separating Joseph and scribes, 102; and blockage in Book of Mormon translation, 106

Smith, Hyrum, 60, 81–82

Smith, Jesse, 82

Smith, Joseph Jr.: and Book of Mormon publication, 1–2; and impact of Book of Mormon, 2–3; as prophet, 3; translation method of, 3–4, 5–6, 62–79, 92–93, 108; revelations given to, 9–10, 48–50; role of, in Restoration, 9–10; spiritual progression and preparation of, 9–14, 23–24, 79, 89, 105–6; financial situation of, 11–12, 14–15, 17, 25, 34, 48; transgressions of, 11–12, 16; and obtaining gold plates, 11–17, 20–23; courtship with Emma, 18; marriage of, 18–20; and early Book of Mormon translation, 25–35; and lost Book of Mormon manuscript pages, 37–41, 86; recommences work on Book of Mormon translation, 41–43; and Marin Harris's request to see gold plates, 43–46; and finishing Book of Mormon translation, 48–61; baptism of, 52; and witnesses of gold plates, 57–61; education and writing abilities of, 62–63; and use of seer stones versus Urim and Thummim, 80–84; and translation without seer stones, 84–92; and possible dictation of Book of Mormon, 93–95; and scribes' testimony regarding use of seer stones, 95–98; as possibly creatively involved in Book of Mormon translation, 98–99; and God's translation method, 100; and other translation theories, 101–2; sheet separating scribes and, 102–5; and need for gold plates in translation, 105–7

Smith, Joseph Sr., 13–14, 15, 17, 21, 41, 42, 60

Smith, Lucy Mack: and Smith family's financial situation, 12, 15; on Moroni's visits, 13; on marriage of Joseph and Emma Smith, 18–19; on Joseph's obtaining gold plates, 21–22, 23; on attempts to steal gold plates, 26; on Book of Mormon translation, 26; on lost Book of Mormon manuscript pages, 39–40; visits Emma and Joseph in Harmony, 41; on seer stones, 81

Smith, Samuel, 46–47, 52, 60

"Spectacles," 12–13, 27, 69, 72, 74, 81–82. *See also* seer stones; Urim and Thummim

Stevenson, Edward, 89–90

Stones. *See* seer stones

Stowell, Josiah, 18

Taves, Ann, 99, 101, 102

Turley, Richard, 75–76

Uchtdorf, Dieter F., 77–78

Urim and Thummim, 12–13, 28–30, 34, 40, 67, 80–84, 85, 88, 90, 91, 92. *See also* seer stones

Visions, in translation process, 97–98

Weed, Thurlow, 1
Welch, John, 101
Whitmer, Christian, 60
Whitmer, David, 46, 55–57,

INDEX

58–60, 67–69, 76, 104–5, 106, 108
Whitmer, Jacob, 60
Whitmer, John, 60
Whitmer, Mary, 56

Whitmer, Peter Jr., 60
Woodruff, Wilford, 74–75, 90, 109

Young, Brigham, 10–11, 75